Critical Thinking 2

Think Harder!

Advanced Analysis Using DontBeStupid.club Principles for Good Decisions

H. Granville James

ITSUS
PRESS

Critical Thinking 2
Think Harder!
Advanced Analysis Using DontBeStupid.club
Principles for Good Decisions

ISBN: 978-1537221854
ISBN-13: 153722185X

Contents

1.
Let's Begin

STUPID (ADJECTIVE) - SHOWING a lack of thought or good judgment.

Critical Thinking (noun) – The objective analysis and evaluation of an issue, question or situation in order to form a judgement. (verb) The act of really doing it.

Everyone understands the noun, but not many commit to the verb.

Critical thinking is the smart person's weapon against stupidity. If enough of us do some critical thinking every day, we can make the world a little less stupid.

Hopefully all that sounds familiar. Our first book on Critical Thinking, "Don't Be Stupid about Critical Thinking", tries very hard to make those points. And we really hope you've read that book already. We consider Book One "the basics" on critical thinking. Those 11 principles are our foundation.

(By the way, we *italicize* our principles when using them in our writing. Kind of like the light in the carwash that tells you it's "waxing now"...)

We have way too much information to process today. There's no way we can know everything we are expected to know plus everything we want to know. It creates urgency. Everyone is in a hurry. We rush through everything. All those decisions, everything we must get done today, there's never enough time. We must go faster and faster. It's a stampede.

And then we start making mistakes. Little ones at first, but they add up. And if we don't pay attention to those warning signs, if we don't stop and take control, then we make bigger mistakes. And then we get trapped… we never catch up, we never have time to enjoy life. It just goes on and on. All because we did not commit to critical thinking.

Time is Precious. It just goes on and on all right, but for only a little while. Then it's over. Pow! That was your life. Blink and you missed it. We rushed through it, never took time to think about most of it, and maybe worst of all, we made a lot of stupid decisions. Instead of a great life, meh…

Why? Who decided this should be my life?

Life doesn't have to be that way. You can step away from the herd. Jump out anytime and start a life guided by critical thinking.

You can choose your way to a great life.

And that's all we're going to say about "why". It should be enough. The world doesn't need another book with half the pages telling you why critical thinking is good or what it does for you.

We all know the value of good decisions. If you ask people, you will get 100% the same answer. Everyone would like to make good decisions. *Time is Precious.* You don't need more sales pitch. What would be useful is to help people really do some critical thinking.

Our books assume you want to think critically. We explore how we really do it.

Book One, "Don't Be Stupid about Critical Thinking", introduces our thinking system and offers a framework for making good decisions. It's the starting point. By design, it must start at the beginning and end somewhere. But the potential for critical thinking is infinite. Our capacity for better decision-making is limited only by the time we can devote to critical thinking. And we can do a lot more than just get started.

But don't underestimate the power of the basics. Our principles are easy to comprehend, but most people never master using those "simple" tools. Book One is enough to make you a pretty good critical thinker if you really use it. *First Things First.* You have to walk before you can run.

Now it's time to advance.

This book builds on the basics. This material is useful on its own, but you will get more benefit if the basics are firmly in place first. Let's use this point as our first example of some simple critical thinking here in this book.

There Will Be Math – You are going to spend your time. Get the most return on your investment. Read the books in order. Practice the basics until they are a habit. And always remember hubris is the enemy of critical thinking.

But now it's time to take our principles to the next level. We are going to explore some more challenging critical thinking. And don't worry, it should never be too hard. Everything builds on what comes before.

There is no such thing as a "quick-thinker". Every healthy brain works very quickly. Everyone thinks much faster than they can speak the words to describe what they're thinking. No one is a "quick thinker" just because they're always ready to speak. The slowest brain is moving many times faster than the quickest mouth.

Speaking is a great equalizer. It slows everyone down to a speed where everyone can keep up. No one else can speak as quickly as you can think. And thinking is where it all starts.

Critical thinking is like any other motor skill. You start out bumbling your way through it. But with practice you get very good at it. Just like riding a bicycle. Or swimming. Or driving a manual transmission.

Ever watch a skilled operator run a backhoe? The scoop acts like an extension of their arm. They weren't that good on their first day. But after enough practice, the skills become automatic. You want critical thinking skills to be like that shovel, an automatic extension of yourself.

There's a little irony there, but it's true. Good critical thinking becomes something you do automatically, without thinking. If you give it enough practice, your brain works the same way that operator swings the shovel around. Knock down a few stupid statements and people start calling you a quick-thinker. But you already know, you're really a critical thinker.

As we discussed in Book One, our basic thinking process uses 11 Principles. Using any one of them will improve your answer. If you use two on a problem, you will get a better answer. Two means you have 121 possible combinations. Three? That's 1,331 possibilities. And if you go all the way to 11, you have over 285 billion ways to attack a problem with critical thinking. I can't imagine a question needing all that, but it feels good to know all that's available.

More complex decisions become as easy as basic ones after a little practice. Everything builds on what came before. The potential for progress is infinite. Time is the only limit.

There are a lot of real-world examples in this book. We want to illustrate critical thinking using familiar subjects. Some examples are very simple to make a point clear.

And some examples don't have clear answers. Some of those examples might be challenging emotionally. *Don't Be Distracted.* The point is to exercise critical thinking. We intend no offense when our point of view sneaks through. But *Open Mind* is our most important principle, and challenging our emotions is something an advanced critical thinker does every day. It's how you learn. There is never any growth if you cannot change your mind.

If you become an advanced critical thinker, then it's inevitable - you will change your mind on many topics. Maybe more than once. And that's the whole point, isn't it? New information comes along all the time. A critical thinker always wants to find the best answers. Enough good answers and you make your life great.

You have to commit to being a critical thinker. You

have to actually do it, over and over again. So please don't skip the "getting in shape" chapter. Getting started is more important than anything else. It will sound too easy. Try to really do it.

Some of the discussions get a little long; it's advanced critical thinking. But we've also included some brief interludes and habits you can adopt quickly. We hope you travel deeper into the analysis with us in all the long chapters, but even just the short interludes will serve to advance your critical thinking skills.

OK, time to advance. Let's think harder!

2.
Interlude: Habit #1

FIRST THINGS FIRST. This is a good habit for making the most efficient use of your time. And more time is a benefit that helps everything else in your life. Any habit that impacts the rest of your life deserves a high priority.

Define the Target. Intellectually Dishonest. – Failure to apply information and standards of evaluation of which one is aware; inclusion of irrelevant data in an effort to confuse or in some way hinder progress toward a rational conclusion. Applying different standards of judgment to circumstances based on achieving a predesigned outcome. *Simplify.* This wastes a critical thinker's time.

Define the Target. Intellectually Honest – Considering facts in an equally unbiased manner; using all relevant data and not purposefully omitting data that would lead to a different conclusion. *Simplify.* This helps a critical thinker learn and grow.

In any discussion, it is intellectually honest to point out errors or omissions in facts or logic. Intellectually honest people want the right answer, and it's easy for them to eliminate mistakes without regard to who made the mistake or its impact on the outcome. Intellectually honest people are after the shortest path to the best answer.

Pretty much everything else that enters a discussion or debate is intellectually dishonest. All tactics seeking to confuse, obfuscate, distract, etc. they're all dishonest. None of them is motivated toward helping a discussion reach the best answer. Their intention is to persuade toward a desired outcome when the facts alone are not enough to make the answer clear.

This is why the term "political debate" is always an oxymoron. I have never seen an intellectually honest debate between politicians. It's always about supporting preconceived outcomes and trying to persuade everyone else to believe. More often than not, they all suck. None is as good as the average preacher.

Intellectually honest people are committed to the *Open Mind* principle. Perhaps the most useful habit a critical thinker can adopt is avoiding the dishonest and only spending time with intellectually honest people. Life is just more efficient that way.

Time is Precious. We seek out intellectually honest people, and we minimize time spent with the intellectually dishonest. *Simplify.* Bullshit wastes our time.

3.
Get in Critical Thinking Shape

DEFINE THE TARGET – Critical Thinking. The objective analysis and evaluation of an issue, question or situation in order to form a judgement. We explored the "noun" side of this definition in Book One, "Don't be Stupid about Critical Thinking". Now let's talk more about the verb, really doing it.

First Things First. We have to get in shape. And you can begin this fitness program without consulting your physician.

Thinking is our most repeated habit. We are always thinking. The methods used and the patterns laid down are repeated over and over. Some estimates say you have 50,000 or more thoughts per day. There's not much hard data on that for a critical thinker to really embrace, so let's just use it as a generalization to help make this point:

We are always thinking.

Habits are formed by repetition, and you will be thinking thousands of times every day. Thinking habits are formed very quickly. And that means they can also be changed very quickly. Old thinking habits can be broken and replaced with new and improved habits very quickly. It just takes commitment.

Let's begin our fitness program with a little motivation.

Most of us start life as good critical thinkers. Humans learn very quickly during their first few years of life. And they learn objectively. There's no emotion involved in life's earliest lessons. You eat and avoid pain. You learn to walk. It all happens very quickly and objectively. You were a critical thinking superstar when you were two years old. But the rest of the world has other plans.

Once we're old enough, the world starts trying to take what it wants from us. *Follow the Money*. Most of our interaction with the world is based on some kind of trade. You want something, and it wants something. And so the bullshit begins! Once we get old enough, the world starts turning us into poor thinkers because that's how they get more from us. The worse your thinking powers, the more you lose.

The process of corrupting your thinking starts before you're aware of it, long before you're in control of your own thinking. It starts when we're too young to know any better. You don't know it's happening. But you spend most of your childhood getting trained to think the way other people want you to think.

And here is the most important point for motivation today: **When you think the way other people want you to think, then you've been trained to give them what they want.** If you don't *Think for Yourself* then you're just another puppy sitting and speaking on command. Good boy! Here's your biscuit.

The path through your childhood is chosen by other people. You have no choice. Someone else makes all those decisions for you. You are trained by them to think however they want you to think.

As you reach adulthood, there is another path laid out in front of you. This path leads all the way until you die. And this path also was laid out for you by someone else. But there is one big difference. No one can force you to stay on this path. Now you do have a choice. You can step away from the herd.

Follow the Money. When other people choose your path, their best interests are considered first. That's not good enough for a critical thinker. We choose our way to our best life. And that's not going to be the same as someone else's choices for us.

So one day, hopefully, you wake up and decide you don't like the path you're on. You realize all these choices are someone else's idea. You decide it's time to *Think for Yourself* and make your life something better. You may not know the name for it yet, but you're about to do some Critical Thinking!

Hurray! Emancipation from the tyranny of conditioning... Now what?

Well, that's why we're here. Consider us a spirit guide for people who don't believe in spirits. Critical thinking guides our path through life. And it's time to flex those brain muscles.

Using critical thinking is very similar to getting in shape physically. The hardest part is getting started. But if you get going and remain committed, one day you realize your brain can run a marathon and has the equivalent of "six-pack" abs. It's that tangible. You know the answers and you can feel it.

If you're getting in shape physically, you can run a few miles or do an hour or two of lifting per day. That's about all you can handle physically. You might even need recovery days too. If you're old enough - ahem - you need a recovery day after every exercise day.

But we think all day, every day, seven days a week. Age doesn't matter. Non-stop thinking with no recovery days.

There Will Be Math – Three days of thinking is the equivalent of about 6 weeks training to get in shape physically. That assumes you train for an hour a day or think for 14 hours a day. (you can even get crazy and think while you run if you want.)

So, you want fast results in your exercise programs? You can commit to being a critical thinker in the morning, and by evening you will be in reasonable shape. One day and you're already the equivalent of two weeks into a physical training program.

After a few days, you will be a critical thinker. And with just a little maintenance, the habits will stay with you for life. As an added bonus, you never get injured by thinking. Your career will not be cut short by knee problems or a hip injury. Just avoid hitting your head really hard and your thinking career will last a lifetime.

To get started, make your commitment. Pick a day when you are ready to commit, draw a line in the sand, and resolve to never make a stupid decision again. That's harder than it sounds. Life makes it very easy to avoid thinking. Just follow the path with the rest of the herd. We get very lazy without realizing it.

All those decisions without thinking are not necessarily

bad, but someone else is making them and your benefit is second to theirs. Sometimes you gain a little, sometimes you lose a lot. Either way, the bigger dog is eating first. You are not choosing your best possible life.

OK, we're not going to be a lazy thinker anymore. Getting started will take some commitment, so make sure you don't quit smoking or do something else difficult on the same day. Critical thinking starts out harder than it looks. But it also gets easier very quickly. You're just getting in shape.

It starts with our 11 principles in Book One. Those are the tools we use to find our answers.

Answers last a long time. Some last a lifetime. You do not need to answer the same questions over and over. Critical thinking makes your life very efficient, but only if you make good decisions. Everything builds on the previous answers, so you have to get them right. Just like with physical training, an injury can cost you a lot of time.

Going slowly in the right direction is far better than quickly going wrong. The very first step of critical thinking is to take your time and make the right decision. Quality is all that matters. Quantity will take care of itself.

So let's get started on a sample day. It will be easy to play along and fill in your own day. This will sound ridiculously simple. And that trap can stop you from ever being a good critical thinker. Hubris kills critical thinking. Universally, everyone thinks they understand more than they really do. That's stupid.

OK, you've been warned. Let's start our first new day.

Today we commit to being a critical thinker. Start the moment you wake up. Why are we getting up right now? What's the deal? Is it worth it? Possible answer: "it's Saturday, I could sleep in but I'm not tired anymore. I want to read a little and I'm looking forward to coffee." That is an acceptable critical thinking reason to get out of bed. So is "I really need to pee".

Unacceptable answers include: "it's when I always get up; it's when someone else wants me to get up; the alarm went off; I have too much to do today", and anything similar. Those are programming, not objective answers to the fundamental question.

There Will Be Math. Why are you getting up? What do you get in exchange for getting up?

Lay in bed until you work out an objective reason for getting up. Understand, you will not have to do this every morning, because every time a situation repeats when you already know the answer, time is saved. And today, you have started critically thinking about your life. So it starts when you wake up. Before you get out of bed this morning, you are already thinking about "why" you do it. Knowing that answer may even change some of your decisions today. Tomorrow morning the "why" may be a little easier question if you make your life better today.

By the way, if you objectively conclude life sucks and there's really no good reason to get out of bed, that's a legitimate critical thinking conclusion. It really is, as long as it's based on objective analysis of facts. In that case, use this reason to get your motor running: "I have to make some changes in my life and I can't do it while staying in bed". And then be excited to get up, because you have a big day ahead.

OK, we're finally out of bed. Yay! Critical thinking almost stopped us but we made it. Now think critically about each item that touches you in that first hour out of bed. Likely first stop, the bathroom. Do you like your toothpaste, toilet paper, towels, soap, showerhead, water quality, etc.? Is everything you touch the best possible choice?

There has to be an objective reason or else you're just doing it without thinking. That is the habit we're breaking. In the first hour you're awake, most people will encounter at least 10 things that are not really optimized. They bought them because someone else convinced them, or they're just following a ritual because it's always been that way. Critical thinkers can do better.

First Things First. Don't skip this first hour because it sounds too simple. This is practice. It's the lay-up drill before the basketball game. Don't skip it until you're doing it on auto-pilot.

My morning ritual includes my favorite everything. Actually, just my coffee is enough reason to get out of bed any day. But the right showerhead makes 1.5 GPM luxurious, and you can't beat Dr. Bronner's soaps. As a pathological critical thinker, I even have the best sources for everything. Much of it auto-ships from Amazon. And by taking the time to make all those great decisions, they all repeat on auto-pilot now.

All of that is simple. Confucius would be proud and it

doesn't take a genius to do it. But it takes some critical thinking. You don't just want something, you know "why" and you know it's your best choice. That's critical thinking.

Consider this. *First Things First.* If you love everything that touches you in that first hour of every day, from your morning shower to your breakfast routine, how much happier would you start every day? Forget about saying something positive into the mirror, the right toothpaste, and my Sonic Care toothbrush are far more powerful affirmations.

Maybe you already have your first hour perfected too? Great! But do the analysis one more time anyway. Just ask "Why?". Then ask "Is it worth it?". And finally, ask "Can I do better?". Do that for everything you do in that first hour after waking up. Let's abbreviate that as the "WIC" analysis for our convenience.

Why? Is it worth it? Can I do better? WIC.

This process will be annoying at first. It slows you down. And we always have to be in a rush, right? Everything must be fast so we can... so we can what? (rushing is a stupid idea, we'll attack it later.) Critical thinking is not about speed, it's about quality. A few good decisions are worth far more to your quality of life than a lot more bad decisions.

If you really do it, by the end of the first hour of the first day, the WIC thought process will start becoming a habit. You might even be having fun with it. Just keep doing it over and over. Eventually, it will start happening on its own. A new habit.

End of hour one. Congratulations! You just did your first

3-mile jog for your brain. And you don't need a recovery day. You don't even need to take a break. We can go right on into the second hour.

Let's pause here and say a few words about "mindfulness" or "being present". These are hot topics today. Being a critical thinker is the ultimate form of mindfulness. We are very aware of our circumstances. And we are more than just "present" or "in the moment". We are using all that awareness to make choices that optimize those moments.

I'm very interested in "being present" in my best possible life. And I won't settle for being present or mindfully-aware of a mediocre life. Become a great critical thinker and you'll never worry about your "mindfulness" again.

Now for the rest of our first critical thinking day, just make sure you objectively think about every decision point you can. "WIC" for everything you have time to think about. **W**hy? **Is** it worth it? **C**an I do better? WIC.

Don't wear yourself out, but try to think critically about any decision that seems worth it at the time. You're getting in shape. You rest whenever you need to. Not many have the stamina for all day the first day.

As you go through the day, always remember; decisions that repeat are the most important. Prioritize those. You need the best answers because they will repeat over and over. *There Will Be Math*. The cumulative impact of a repeating decision is the real value of that decision. It may seem like one little thing today, but if it happens 1,000 times, you get the results 1,000 times. Something very little ends up 1,000 times bigger. One cigarette, no big deal... but 1,000? You will feel it. Anything that repeats is a candidate for the cigarette test.

Let's put an example into our first day. We said today is Saturday. Maybe that's grocery shopping day. We'll assume the "WIC" on that idea is already done, grocery shopping today is our best choice, so now we're driving to the store. Should you pass that car ahead of you? This question will repeat almost every time we drive. "WIC" time.

There Will Be Math. We're passing to get there faster; we save time. Calculate how much time you gain. If you're 5 miles from your exit on an expressway, it will take you 5 minutes at 60 MPH. Can you go 70 MPH if you pass that slowpoke? Then you will save about 30 seconds. So **W**hy? To get there sooner. **Is** it worth it? You gain 30 seconds. **C**an I do better? This is where we can get a little advanced.

If you want to advance your critical thinking, *There Will Be Math*. You have to know the ROI, the return on your investment. You're getting 30 seconds, but what is being invested? Can you make a better investment with the same resources?

There is more investment to pass that car than just tapping the accelerator. You also must include some allowance for the increased chances of an accident. It might be only one in a million, but the cost is potentially huge. You must also consider whatever additional fuel you burn with the acceleration. Your car is roughly 10 times more fuel-efficient cruising steadily than while accelerating to pass. One time does not add much, but if you make the choice to pass every time, then no question you are spending more on fuel.

And finally, how about added stress from being in a rush? Why? So you can get to the store and spend faster? Relax. Being in a hurry is someone else's idea.

This is an idea we will attack over and over. The world wants you to be in the habit of rushing. *There Will Be Math*. The more things you do, the more chances to get something from you. Rushing around without "WIC" thinking is a bad habit. If you do the critical thinking, you will find very few things that really mean that much to you.

Most people pass slower cars without thinking about it. A certain percentage even express their frustration at the slower driver. The world trained them to do this. There's no critical thinking involved. Everyone just needs to get somewhere ASAP, right? If we go faster we can get more done.

But now you've decided to *Think for Yourself*. You're making an objective decision. So "WIC". Add it all up. Why are you rushing? Is it worth it? Rushing around and being stressed is a lousy way to spend a day. It's rarely ever worth it to a critical thinker. Stress is a killer. Slowing down and making good decisions is how you reduce stress in your life.

I'll add a personal note here. I never pass in this circumstance and have discovered an added benefit to that choice. If you're driving behind the slower car, you get the full entertainment value of watching people pass and observing their state of mind.

Some are just in a hurry and they're kind of boring.

Some are talking on the phone, which is both illegal and dangerous so you know there's no critical thinking going on over there, plus you know to avoid them if you see them later. But the most entertaining are people who are angry at the slower driver. And, it looks like they assume the slower driver will be interested in their opinion too.

Moments like these can help you appreciate life. You can't help but be thankful you're a critical thinker. Life is harder for stupid people...

Once you've done this traffic exercise, you have your answer. If you drive a lot, this question will come up a lot. But you don't ever have to think about the answer again. Every time this situation arises, you already have your answer. It's a habit. In my case, you just cruise along behind the slower car for the next 5 minutes, enjoy the show, and think about something else.

Who knows what else you might think about during all that "bonus" time. Eventually you will think about something else that makes your life better. And now your good decision is compounding. Time saved from one good decision was available to make another good decision.

Over and over again. Critical thinking gives you the power to take control of your life and make it better. Situations repeat, you already have the answer, and you use that time to think about something else. The power grows exponentially. The more you use it, the more answers are resolved, and that means more time for new thinking. The potential is infinite.

Over and over again, into infinity. As that idea sinks in, it should begin to focus awareness on how important it is to get all those recurring decisions right.

Do not fall into the trap of thinking it sounds too simple. Anything less than the best answer is going to compound every time you do it. And anything you are doing without understanding "why" is probably not making your life the best possible life.

Continue this type of exercise throughout the first day. As much as you can handle. Now tonight, when you lay down to sleep, think about the day. Don't mindlessly drift off thinking about a TV show. Think about the choices you made and see if any of them stand out. What were your best ones? Those are the ones that will get you out of bed faster tomorrow morning.

OK, end of day one. That's the brain training equivalent of two weeks running to get in shape. If you really did it for most of the day, then congratulations. You are already doing more critical thinking than 95% of the people you meet every day.

Now let's get up tomorrow and do it again!

Don't Be Distracted. Critical thinking doesn't start with answering big problems or solving the world's big crises. Most people out there trying to act smart, they get it wrong most of the time. There's not a lot of critical thinking on display, but there is a lot of pseudo-intellectualism. They probably want to make better decisions. They just don't know how.

Here's what will happen as you concentrate on your daily choices. As the basics become habit, you will begin to think about the bigger problems in the same way. Instead of being overwhelmed by emotion or rhetoric, or giving some pre-programmed response, you will be in the habit of breaking questions down with objective analysis. No problem is too big to think about when you have the tools in place to do it.

Lay down a solid foundation for your life. The more often a decision repeats, the more important it is that you've locked in the best possible answer.

Getting started is simple. But so is running. And you are not in shape until you can run the distance. Understanding critical thinking is not enough. You have to really do it.

Get in Critical Thinking shape!

4.
Finding Answers Means a Really Open Mind

DEFINE THE TARGET. Critical Thinking – The objective analysis and evaluation of an issue, question or situation in order to form a judgment.

Open Mind – A willingness to consider new ideas.

New ideas are required to make your life better.

Critical thinking is a method for answering questions. But it's not the only method. Answers are everywhere. Most questions have too many answers available. They're easy to find and, in most cases, it's easier to just look up an answer than it is to think about it.

Google has been great for many reasons, but it's been terrible for critical thinking. It makes us lazy. People can find any answer they want. But search engines find the most popular answers, and the size of an audience has nothing to do with accuracy.

"I wish you idiots would stop misquoting me on the Internet."

~ Albert Einstein

All those entertaining answers won't make your life better. Only the right answers can do that. You need critical thinking to find the best answers. Accepting the right answer instead of the popular answer requires an *Open Mind.*

People work very hard to believe what they want to believe. And the harder they work to believe it, the worse they make their life. The easiest way to distract many people is to just tell them what they want to hear.

In most cases, you can think whatever you want and muddle through life. But it's terribly inefficient and the decisions repeat. The more inefficiency that piles up, the harder life gets. Most people reach a point where they have no more capacity. They can't find new answers because they have to expend so much energy working with the wrong ones they're already using. And that's it for their life. There's no capacity left for anything more.

The lack of an *Open Mind* is the single biggest obstacle to choosing your best possible life. Wanting to believe something is irrelevant. The right answer does not change based on emotions.

A critical thinker has an easier life. The amount of energy stupid people waste trying to live with their wrong answers could be used to make their lives better. A critical thinker with an *Open Mind* has all that extra time available.

Using our driving example from the previous chapter, just that one answer gives the critical thinker at least 100 additional opportunities a year to think about something else to make their life better (assumes twice a week for 50 weeks, and reality is probably many more times than that...). Just based on this one right answer, the critical thinker has 100 more opportunities to think about something else. Just another example of the efficiency gained from critical thinking.

If you began your critical thinking journey before the internet age (as I did) then today is an amazing time to be alive. Never has so much knowledge been available so quickly and easily. The idea of sitting at your desk and learning about anything you want, and the only effort required being to tap a keyboard? It's almost ridiculous. If you ever had to go to a library to learn about something, you know what I mean. There's really no excuse for stupidity today.

With that kind of potential at everyone's fingertips, you can't help but wonder why the world is so stupid. There's more than one reason, but the most troublesome answer is too many people have stopped thinking critically. That reason is 100% under our own control. People don't have to be stupid. But the world just makes it too easy to stop thinking. *There Will Be*

Math. Lazy thinking equals stupidity.

People look up answers. And they find ones they like. But that's not objective analysis and it's not research. You have to review facts and verify answers if you want to be a critical thinker.

Example: The cholesterol test says 260. The doctor recommends a statin drug. The patient goes home and Googles. They "confirm" it. With total cholesterol of 260, the recommendation is a statin drug. Now they feel better about themselves for researching it and they take the drug.

And that's just stupid. What was done is not analysis. That is recycling the same information. Finding something else that says the same thing they got from the doctor. That's not critical thinking. It's just wasting time.

A critical thinker will analyze data. "WIC". **W**hy? What does the number 260 mean? Quantify what it really means to my health. Then, what is the cost of statin drug therapy? **I**nclude money and side effects too. **I**s it worth it? And finally: **C**an I do better?

Yes, this is much harder and will take more time than the simple "confirmation" done above. But since you're going to repeat this decision daily for the rest of your life, and *Respect Nature* since you will be taking a drug that alters what your body is doing naturally, you really need to be sure it's the best decision. Slow down and use critical thinking to make the best decision. (we'll analyze this question in depth as one of our "real world" examples later in this book.)

But it's easier to just hear the answer you want, go fast

and trust other people's decisions for you. And what follows is a lot of stupidity. Bad answers get repeated over and over until they become "true". And the herd moves closer to the edge of the cliff.

We have infinite information available, but no guarantee any of it is accurate. In fact, the most certain way to gain an audience is to ignore facts and tell people what they want to hear. That works fine for entertainment, but it's a terrible way to learn about important decisions.

For example, I loved Jon Stewart's show along with millions of other people. But he is an entertainer. He is not objective. And his facts are frequently wrong. That's not a problem when the point is to be funny. But when you start reading Jon Stewart is the most trusted newsman in America... well, that means it's time to worry a little about the state of critical thinking.

Finding the right answers instead of popular answers is an advanced concept lesson for the *Open Mind* principle. Do not accept answers because you like them. Verify with an *Open Mind*. You must learn the truth whether or not you like it.

Now let's advance further. Add *Don't Be Distracted.* Identify the people telling you what you want to hear. Anyone telling you what you want to hear has something to gain by doing it. For a laugh, maybe it's OK. For a drug therapy, probably not.

Advance further. Now *Follow the Money*. Now you know someone is trying to manipulate your answer, what is their motive? What do they gain from it?

At first glance, that above sequence might look like a

lot of thinking. Well, it really is. It's more than most people will ever do. But that's how advanced critical thinking works. You keep drilling down until you're satisfied you really understand the situation and have the best answer.

But here's the thing. Your brain works very fast. And thinking this way gets easy if you do it over and over. It becomes a habit. It happens automatically. The situation repeats over and over and you deal with it automatically. You are no longer manipulated by someone telling you what you want to hear. In fact, you skip all the way to the end and see why they're doing it. For the rest of your life. You're such a quick thinker... because you practiced it.

Most people won't put in the effort to get good at it. People choose the immediate gratification from hearing what they want to hear. It's just easier. And then they go wherever the bullshit takes them. Easy, but it's not their decision and it won't be their best possible life.

Returning to our Jon Stewart example, the distraction and its purpose are harmless. Maybe even beneficial. It's good for everyone when intelligent entertainers get good ratings. And laughing is good for you too. But you do have to remember it's entertainment.

When the time comes for meaningful decisions, it's no time for entertainment. Objective analysis is needed to choose your best life. The best answer is always the goal. Love it or hate it, emotions have nothing to do with it.

5.
Counterintuitive Decisions

COUNTERINTUITIVE DECISIONS REQUIRE our *Open Mind* to override *Common Sense* in order to reach the best answer. A simple example might be vaccinations. It seems wrong to put a disease into your body, and it really seems wrong to let someone stick you with a needle. But sometimes vaccinations are good for you. Google polio if you need an example.

Another example: many injured areas tend to grow back stronger than they were before. Weightlifters know this is how muscle is added. But it's also true of most bones. Stressing your bones may sound wrong, but it prevents loss of bone density. Don't go crazy, just jump around occasionally...

And antacids don't cure heartburn. Neutralizing your stomach acid tends to make the problem worse.

Those are some easy examples. They're only a little counterintuitive. Now let's step it up to a level worthy of an advanced critical thinker.

I love maggot therapy for this example. Is there anything more counter-intuitive than pouring maggots into an open wound? Yuck.

But maggots eat infected tissue and they excrete anti-microbial residue back out. They are a living organism, eating and then eliminating, going about the business of survival just like you do. But they eat rotting organic matter and they excrete cleaning fluid. Amazing. *Respect Nature*. You simply can't do as good a job with any topical disinfectants or systemic drugs made by humans. Maggots are alive and looking for their food. Added bonus, they are the ultimate locavore.

One more added benefit, and this one gets bigger every day, maggots don't care if the infection is antibiotic resistant or not. They eat it the same way.

Ok. We'll stop the maggot discussion now because it's a little yucky. But it's true. And if it's the best decision for healing, then a critical thinker will want it. Unfortunately, maggot therapy is so counterintuitive you probably won't get it even when you should. *Open Mind* is not practiced enough in the world of Western medicine. But if your wound is not healing and they're trying yet another antibiotic on you, it might be time to *Think for Yourself* and speak up.

Let's look at a more everyday example that's a little less visceral. You are considering two new houses at the same price in the same neighborhood. One is 20% bigger and has a much larger back yard. Same price, more house, so no-brainer right? Go big.

Getting less of anything for the same price is a counterintuitive decision. Most of the time, we automatically choose to get "more" for our money. But purchase cost is only one variable in a critical thinking analysis. If you stop and think objectively, there may be many reasons you're better off with a smaller house. Utility costs, landscaping, furnishings, maintenance, etc. Ultimately, unless you really need the extra space, it's almost a certainty the smaller house is your better choice even though it costs just as much.

A similar example is food. You are always better off with the smaller sized soda pop. Yes, for only a few cents more you can get enough to float a small boat, but it's bad for you. Getting more is not a great value, even if it's free.

Most of the time *Trust Common Sense* and you will be correct. But remember, this principle is used as a guide and confirmation of your more objective analysis. You always must be open to finding counterintuitive answers. They are the hardest to find, but sometimes they are the most useful. In the world of medicine, sometimes they can save your life.

In general, anytime you *Think for Yourself* and ignore a consensus opinion, you are starting down the path of a counterintuitive decision. Depending on your respect for public opinion, you may find yourself seeking out counterintuitive answers more and more. In many areas, public opinion is wrong more often than right. Let's do a few more simple examples.

Adding fat into your diet to lose weight is counterintuitive. Yet numerous studies have shown just adding olive oil into your diet causes some weight loss. Let's not get into the science of it here, but eating fat makes you thin? Counterintuitive.

Eating foods high in cholesterol does not raise your cholesterol. This is so counter-intuitive, an entire industry was born around reducing cholesterol. *Follow the Money.* Egg substitute (fake eggs) is still a huge product category. Ever look at the ingredient list on zero-cholesterol egg substitutes? Yuck... But it sounded logical. You need to lower your cholesterol and this egg substitute has no cholesterol in it.

You know what? Critical thinkers never worried about eating eggs. There never was any data, just an idea that sounded logical. But critical thinkers are already aware of counterintuitive answers. A statement sounding logical is only the very beginning. Objective analysis will frequently reveal a counterintuitive answer.

In fact, the actual data on eggs always indicated the opposite of the logical sounding theory. Egg-eaters were just as healthy as no-egg people in every study. No study ever showed a link between egg consumption and anything unhealthy. But some studies showed higher rates of death among the subjects who ate no eggs.

And now some studies show higher rates of death among statin users. Counterintuitive?

Now that you're a critical thinker, you will always be on the lookout for ideas that sound good but don't have any facts supporting them. Usually, they will involve someone else benefitting. The cholesterol scare was not innocent. It's still generating billions in profits for the wrong people. (We will revisit this example later.)

Most counterintuitive decisions get that way due to our socialization. Maggot therapy is a good example. There are places on earth where people don't go "yuck" over that idea. Cholesterol worry is another. A critical thinker has to beware of socialized behaviors. Someone else made those decisions. And they were not thinking about your best interests when they did it. Those kinds of answers are just the herd moving together. While everyone else might just accept something as "right", a critical thinker must know "why".

Let's look at one more example under this heading. This one affects everyone working to pay their bills.

"Saving" in a 401K for a retirement 30 or 40 years away is a bad decision for most people. Using data available at your fingertips, you can prove this for yourself. Or you can read our money and investing books. You can do much better things with your money. Doing that is a counterintuitive decision now, and there are a lot of people working to make it feel that way.

Even scarier, government is starting to institutionalize the behavior. Laws are being enacted to "help" you do this saving. It's almost a sacred cow now; nobody is asking "why". Everyone should just start saving for retirement as early as possible. Critical thinkers run the risk of sounding crazy by challenging it. Well...

Think for Yourself. Let's not just accept this idea; let's analyze it with critical thinking.

The theory you are asked to accept is this: you need to save for 30 years so you have enough money to retire and then not work for roughly your last 25 years of life. And you need to do it in your 401K or IRA or MYRA or some other government sanctioned tax-deferred vehicle.

First problem, *Think for Yourself*. Someone else defined that life plan and that goal for you. Do you even want to work for the next 30 years and then not work for 25 more? I know it was never my plan. There are so many fallacies with the concept it's hard to pick a starting point...

But let's use critical thinking to dive in somewhere. *First Things First.* Choose your own path. If someone else chooses, you can be sure it's not with your best interests as the goal. If you are not sure you like this plan for the next 55 years of your life, then just don't do it.

Next, *Don't Be Distracted.* Remember, 401k plans did not exist prior to 1980 (the history is interesting but we won't digress here). So problem number one for a critical thinker, there is no data to prove this is a good idea. This is not something proven successful over multiple generations. It's just some logical sounding statements.

Next, *Follow the Money.* The financial industry was quick to pounce on this windfall of profits and the industry quickly exploded. And now employees everywhere are programmed to "save" in their 401k.

Don't Be Distracted. It's not "saving", it's letting someone else gamble on stocks and bonds using your money. And you pay them, win or lose.

Next, *There Will Be Math.* A dollar today buys about 1/3 what it did 30 years ago. *Trust Common Sense.* Maybe it would have been better to just buy something real and enduring 30 years ago? For example, a new house in the early 1980's was around $80,000. Today it's over $300,000.

The idea that you can save faster than your government devalues the currency is hard to swallow for any critical thinker. *There Will Be Math.* Devaluation is how deficit spending is paid for. Government never makes enough money to pay the bills, but they use inflated dollars in the future to pay back today's debts.

Simplify. When currency is devaluing, saving is stupid. Hard assets accumulation is smart.

Insane levels of government debt mean a lot of devaluation. It's happening now and a lot more is coming. Locking up your money for 30 years in financial assets pretty much guarantees you'll be paying off the debt instead of making your own life better. Buying hard assets that hold their intrinsic value is one way you beat the problem. Like buying that house in 1980.

Next problem: fees. *Follow the Money.* Everyone except you collects a fee from your money. They collect a percentage based on the total, every year, so the longer your money is with them the more fees you pay.

Now *Follow the Money* further. The government is bankrupt. The US government is $20 trillion in debt and projected to go to $30 trillion soon. People cannot even comprehend a trillion dollars. You can say the word, but the brain shuts off when numbers fall outside its normal range of practice.

You know how $20 feels in your pocket. None of us has any concept of what $20 trillion feels like. *Simplify.* The US government needs about $100,000 from every person in the country to pay off its debts. And all indications are that number will keep growing.

Bottom line, the motivation to get you locking up your

money for 30 years has very little to do with your own best interests, and everything to do with covering bills the government cannot pay while also generating obscene profits for a select few people.

As we write this, there is actually a proposal in Congress to create a new government agency to help oversee your retirement savings. *Don't Be Distracted*. Another government department is not the answer. And forcing you to save is just another name for higher taxes.

Simplify. We like George Carlin's guidance here. "I don't believe anything the government tells me. Nothing. Zero." This guidance is actually useful in many questions. There is no other institution where the entire motivation is telling you what you want to hear instead of telling the truth.

There will be some people who believe they can invest so well that they will outperform all those hurdles. OK, if you do the critical thinking analysis and still believe, then maybe you want to feed your 401k for the next 30 years. But at least call it what it is. You're betting you can win the investing game, you're not "saving".

Even without devaluation by external forces, your dollars are not all created equal. *There Will Be Math*. When you have more of something, the value to you of each unit is less. Your first dollars keep you from starving to death, the next ones buy something less important, and eventually you have money to waste. It's less expensive to save when you do it with those surplus dollars. It's a bad decision to save for the future when your dollars are too valuable in the present.

100% of your surplus-dollars is still worth less than one of your needed-dollars.

This means your peak earning years are also the best time to save. Or whenever you have a windfall. The cheapest dollars are the ones you don't need for anything else. Save those whenever they come along. And ignore advice to save 10% of every paycheck.

We got a little deep into the finance of it, so let's return to using it as an example of counterintuitive decision making. Anytime the whole herd starts doing something, it's a good signal to look for counterintuitive answers.

So let's summarize the critical thinking journey on this question. The biggest problem with the whole concept: Whose idea is it that your life consists of 30 years saving and 25 years spending what you saved? *Think for Yourself.* Unless you know what you will want 30 years from now, the idea of depriving oneself today in order to "save for retirement" is just stupid.

And government pressure along with financial industry profits are all about serving their best interests, not yours.

The herd mentality is moving so strongly in the opposite direction, many people's first reaction to this line of thinking is "that's crazy". But really it's just maggot therapy for your retirement plan. It's a counterintuitive answer coming from objective analysis.

Our advertising blurbs say we use critical thinking to choose our best life. This is what we mean. You can choose the same life plan as the rest of the herd. It won't kill you. But it won't be your best possible life.

Very often, counterintuitive decisions are what's needed to get your best life.

6.
Interlude: Habit #2

THIS CRITICAL THINKING habit will haunt your communications forever. Don't start this one unless you're really committed. You have to learn to control it and even hide it sometimes.

As you go through life's interactions, look for extra words added to communications.

As critical thinking disappears, people are using extra words to cover the lack of real substance supporting their statements. It's exactly like the scene in "Back to School" where Thornton Mellon weighs his term paper and then tells his staff "It's too light. It feels like a 'C'. Bulk it up and add a few multi-colored graphs."

That was satire when Rodney Dangerfield did it. Unfortunately, it's real life today. *Don't Be Distracted.* Extra words do not change the objective content of any accompanying information. They are only included to change your evaluation of the information.

Critical thinkers adopt this habit very early. *Don't Be Distracted.* Instead of extra words taking you in their intended direction, your reaction is to analyze why they're being used and then include that motivation when evaluating the information being communicated. Instead of the extra words modifying the information, now you're using the motives of the speaker to modify the information.

First Things First. Before reacting to a communication, notice when unnecessary words are being used.

Normal use of adjectives is not what we're talking about here. A "strong odor" means something different than an "odor". But "exact same" tells you the speaker is trying to make sure you think something is the "same". When I hear "exact same" I immediately look for the differences.

Other redundancies like "honest truth", "convicted felon", "empirical fact", "advance warning", "one single solitary thing" etc. They all point toward added manipulation from the speaker.

Or overly ponderous statements of simpler things. Words like "situation" added where the meaning is already clear, like "emergency situation". Or needlessly long ways of saying something, like "at that one specific moment".

Extra words are everywhere. Make it a habit to spot them. Then, *Don't Be Distracted* by the words. Instead *Follow the Money*. What is the speaker hoping to gain by using extra words? Exactly how intellectually honest or dishonest are they being? Now include that information in your evaluation of their messages.

It might be harmless or it might be nefarious. But frequent use of unnecessary words will alert you that the particular speaker might not have as much substance as they should. Maybe a good use of your time is to listen less as they say more.

And, obviously, pay extra attention in situations where

someone is strongly motivated to persuade you, like selling you something or getting your vote.

Oops, I just did it there by accident. Selling you something and getting your vote are the same thing.

Words deliver a message, and frequently they include information about the speaker in addition to the base message. Using all the information available helps us make better decisions.

7.
Define the Target Better

SELF-TEST FIRST. Avoid the "it's too simple" trap. Especially when you are thinking within your own head, you must define your target. Shortcuts in your head lead to mistakes that are repeated.

A good test is to ask yourself, "How would I explain this to someone else?". If an explanation doesn't quickly pop into your head, then you need to stop and define everything for yourself. Explain it to yourself first. If you really understand it, then explaining it to someone else should be easy.

An easy example would be your spouse asks you to pick up eggs on the way home. Your mutually understood definitions on the subject are defined by your shared shopping history. You both know the request means to buy a one-dozen carton of free-range organic eggs.

That is an easy example, but pause to notice all the possible confusion if the same request was made to someone with no knowledge of your food habits. Number, type and even whether or not they come in a carton are all possible areas of confusion. Someone unfamiliar with English slang might even think they should find the eggs in a field somewhere and pick them up.

Now let's advance this principle to an example that really does confuse people: Does anyone know what "slay" means in 2016?

Define the Target. Slay – To kill a human or animal, usually including dramatic violence.

Slay is literally defined as a dramatic killing. But I'm pretty sure Beyonce doesn't mean to go hunting or kill someone in dramatic fashion when she opens a concert with fans screaming "I slay". So now what?

Well, I know some paranoid white people fear a black uprising. Sorry, just an observation of the world we live in. Google it and you'll find all kinds of Black Panther pictures. (That's the activist group from the sixties, not the animal.) These paranoid people are not using critical thinking, but it is one way to interpret the scene if you assume your definition of "slay" is the agreed meaning.

Let's try to work through it with critical thinking. And yes, I know this isn't terribly important, but the point is to illustrate some critical thinking. If I knew for sure something else was really important to you personally, we would choose that instead. But I happened to read an article that helped feed paranoia, so I was motivated to analyze this. Plus, I like Beyonce.

Ok, slaying. I'm going to slay this...LOL.

First *Trust Common Sense.* Does anyone really think a mega-pop-star and Pepsi spokesperson wants to incite riots or have her fans to go out and kill with violence and drama? Of course not. So clearly the definition is different from the paranoid white people's.

In a slang interpretation, "Kill" also means to do something very well. A comedian whose audience laughed uncontrollably is said to have "killed it". A golfer who set a course record "killed it". So the slang version of "Slay" probably means the same thing as "kill" but with increased drama the same way as in the literal definitions of kill and slay.

"Slay" in 2016 probably means to do something extremely well with added drama, as opposed to just "kill it" which is doing it well but kind of boring in comparison. If Jordan Spieth would light his putter on fire after winning a tournament, then he would "slay" it rather than just "kill" it. I think he'd get more endorsements too.

I don't know Beyonce (to my sorrow...). So this is just my own explanation. I'm not sure it's correct, but at least it's critically thought out.

OK, we're putting too much critical thinking time into concerts and golf. Maybe the point is, don't expect much critical thinking at a concert and just enjoy the show. But if you leave ready to "slay", figure out what it means first. No violence is being encouraged. But I would like to see Jordan ignite a putter once. Would boost the golf ratings for sure.

Defining the Target is always required to reach a mutually agreed conclusion. You cannot agree you've arrived unless you agreed on the destination first.

8.
What and How? First Things First

VIOLATING THE *FIRST* Things First principle leads to good decisions that are not worth very much because they have no impact on your goal. The "drop in an ocean" concept is a good example. It does not help for you to conserve a glass of water while the power plant generating your electricity contaminates a million gallons.

Another good example is if you start any journey in the wrong direction, then every decision afterwards is reduced in value. In simplest terms, if your goal was to the north, and you went south at the start, then it really doesn't matter how great your subsequent decisions are while traveling. The only valuable decision you can make is a U-turn. Go back to the start and begin again.

Any decision that leads to many other decisions requires clear evaluation of *First Things First.* A great life demands correct answers for the decisions having the most impact.

Getting the important decisions right requires a clear understanding of "what" and "how". Goals and ambitions, big dreams, etc. are motivating. They can also be distracting. Knowing the difference is how a critical thinker succeeds.

People get themselves confused with "what" and

"how". A critical thinker sees them as two different concepts. "What" is the goal. "How" is the action used to achieve it. You might observe that Critical Thinking is the "what" and this book is about the "how".

Side note - *Time is Precious*. Try to avoid wasting your time on books that talk too much about "what" and not enough about "how". It should be obvious the goal is shared. That's why you bought the book. Reading 100 pages of why it's good for you is just telling you what you already know. "How" is what you want to read about. That's where the value is in making your life better.

Simple example. Exercise is good for you. That's the "what". And we can write volumes about why it's good for you. All stuff you already know and agree with. It doesn't benefit you too much to just read more of what you already know.

But getting off the couch and walking around the block is a "how". Going to the gym is another "how". Hiring a personal trainer is another "how". Most of the value in your life comes from "how". "What" is important only in making sure you start toward the best goals.

It's quite common for people to agree on a "what" but disagree on the "how". And it's also quite common that confusing the two concepts prevents them from ever making a workable plan. The simplest example of this is any peace talks. People generally agree living conditions are better when they're not at war. Peace is a "What". "How" is obviously a much more difficult question.

A more positive example: the decision to go to the

moon was a really big goal. It inspired a generation and became the life's work for a lot of people. Going to the moon was "what". The "how" is all the work that went into making it happen.

At its best, "what" is a worthy goal. A lot of subsequent decisions are made in pursuit of that goal. Not all of those will be good decisions. It's important to never confuse a decision about "how" with the value of the goal itself. It's all too common to see bad decisions justified because they are pursuing a worthy goal. A bad decision is just bad. It doesn't get any better because the goal is a good one.

The reverse happens too. Some great work is done pursuing poorly chosen goals. It's like our example said at the beginning, any journey must start in the right direction or the value of what follows is greatly reduced. Brilliant moves in pursuit of a bad goal are just wasted.

At its worst, poor and selfish solutions are attached to very worthy goals, and people are tricked into doing great work for the wrong reasons. Critical thinkers separate the "what" from the "how" and see two different questions.

Now to bring this idea up to an advanced critical thinking level, let's look at what happens when we try to solve a real problem. Fix Social Security. That's the "what". Great choice for a goal. Now, "how" to do it? Again, I'll try not to digress into a political discussion.

One of the first "how" answers would be full transparency and public disclosure of data, then followed by people learning more about the issue.

People can't objectively discuss if Social Security is broken or going bankrupt, and politicians scream we need to fix it. People get caught up in the emotions, they scream too, but most people don't know enough to discuss the "how" objectively.

It starts with using real and unemotional data. *There Will Be Math*. People lie about numbers all the time, but numbers themselves always tell a truth. I'm good with numbers. And I'm going to shorten the discussion of this example a little to avoid boring everyone.

The critical thinking answer is Social Security is not as broken as people would like you to think. It makes me crazy every time I hear someone say they "know" it won't be there when they retire. Really? Why do they think they know that? It can't be from critical thinking, that's for sure.

Social Security is not going bankrupt, even in the lifetime of someone starting their first job today. The numbers speak for themselves. Worst case is it will deliver less than today's full benefits. Best case is actually a surplus. And relatively minor tweaks will make big differences. It's really not that big a problem. But it's a great political tool.

Don't Be Distracted. The real problem: all social programs are only as reliable as the government promise to pay. So, in that regard, Social Security is at the same risk as everything else denominated in US dollars and paid by the US government. The payments will be made, but the value of those dollars is certainly at risk. So, rather than singling out Social Security, a critical thinker would rather scream about fixing the economy and eliminating government deficits.

But Social Security works much better as a political tool. It gets people very emotional. *Don't Be Distracted*.

It's good to have goals. "What" gives you something to aim for when you get out of bed in the morning. But allowing yourself to be distracted by distant or improbable decision points wastes your time. It keeps you from thinking about all the things that can make your life better right now. You might envision living next to a mountain stream someday, but getting a water filter today will improve your tap water immediately.

A critical thinker does not allow dreams for tomorrow to get in the way of what must be done today. If you have to feed yourself today, or pay for your kid's school today, you do not save 10% of your paycheck for a retirement dream that's 30 years away. A critical thinker lives in the present and makes their life better every day.

There is no point to putting much effort into any decision when it's not clear if you will ever need it. This is especially true when there are immediate challenges that also require your attention. Choose from what's available right now. *Don't Be Distracted* by later possibilities that do not make your life better today.

And here's the thing. You always live in the present. If you know how to make today great, then today will always be great. There's no reason to dream away about someday when you can actually do something to make today better. Do that every day and the future becomes great.

And here's one more thing. Predicting what you want in

the far off future is a tricky business. The shorter your time frame, the more accurate your predictions.

The practice of making each day great teaches you what really makes your life great. That far off dream will change based on your experiences before you get there.

9.
Interlude: Habit #3

LET'S REVISIT OUR new habit of looking for extra words that try to mislead us.

Oxymorons are fun. Jumbo shrimp, seriously funny, etc. Some are good for a joke.

One hand clapping? Close your eyes in order to see? Some are designed to make you think. Just as often these are designed to make the speaker seem profound.

What about non-dairy creamer? Original copy? Holy war? Some are just designed to sell you something.

Confucius would not be proud. These are all word games that complicate simpler ideas. *Don't Be Distracted*. Laughing is a worthy goal sometimes. But most of the time a critical thinker will reduce an oxymoron down to its real components before including it in any analysis.

Next time you hear about a peace keeper missile or a new tradition, see if you can figure out why someone is describing it that way.

I think my favorite might be non-performing assets. Some of the language coming out of the 2008 financial crisis is just hilarious.

For the record, I use real cream in my coffee. Ever read

the ingredients in non-dairy creamers?

No discussion of oxymorons is complete without mentioning "political solution".

Learn from History. Political solution is always a joke. A critical thinker knows *Don't Be Distracted* and keeps looking for a better answer.

10.
Relativity

AMONG THE MORE iconic TV shows from the 1960's, Star Trek is pretty much in a class by itself. Most people aren't real "Trekkers" or "Trekkies", but we all know what the words mean. Not many people refer to Green Acres or the other giants from that era of television. But Star Trek is with us forever. (*Learn from History*. Star Trek's ratings were terrible. And all those people watching Green Acres missed a cultural event...)

It's often noted that Star Trek lasted only 3 seasons. That's true. But a "season" in the late 1960's was around 26 episodes. You could say people really got their money's worth from television shows back then. So it's true there were only three seasons of Star Trek, but there are 79 one-hour episodes.

Let's relate that to another iconic TV show, Seinfeld. There are 180 Seinfeld episodes. *There Will Be Math*. Without commercials, each Star Trek is about 50 minutes long. Each Seinfeld, about 22 minutes. There are approximately 3950 total minutes of Star Trek and 3960 minutes of Seinfeld.

I'm pausing here to let that sink in. It's a little interesting, isn't it? Hmm, maybe I really am a Trekkie. Anyway...

The point is to illustrate relativity while mentioning two

of my favorite TV shows. Nothing too deep here. It's just a simple example, relativity can be used to guide people's thinking. In this case, they're two unrelated TV shows separated by 20 years. Maybe I want you to think Star Trek is as culturally important as Seinfeld. Or maybe I want you to think TV shows that give you 10 episodes in a season are lazy.

Or maybe I just wanted to make you aware that binge watching Seinfeld or Star Trek will take the same amount of time either way. So you see, critical thinking really can go where no one has gone before.

But the real point is to show how a critical thinker uses relativity to make a point clearer. Many concepts exist somewhere out there in undefined and unlimited space. We use relativity to make them into something everyone can relate to.

And speaking of infinity, humans live within pretty well-defined parameters. Numbers have no boundaries, but our use of numbers tends to be pretty restricted. And when numbers move outside those boundaries, our brains just start thinking of them as "really big" or "really small". We lose the relativity between numbers once they get outside our typical range of use.

We all know when we have "a lot" of money in our wallet. We might even comprehend a million dollars pretty well. How about a billion? And virtually no one really comprehends a trillion dollars. It's just a "really big" number of dollars.

The total US government debt is over $19 trillion right now. It sounds like a big debt. Is it? A critical thinker needs to know more than "sounds big!". That's just an emotional reaction. And normally, whoever is telling you about the debt is trying to make you feel a certain way about it. Critical thinking demands facts, we don't want to feel anything emotional without a good reason.

For a critical thinker, $19 trillion in debt can be neither good or bad until we know what it means. *There Will Be Math*. Our shortest path to understanding this debt goes like this. The US government collects taxes from the people and spends money on behalf of those people. A government's bills and its debts are paid by the people.

If you are an adult citizen of the USA, your share of the debt is about $150,000. We can all comprehend that pretty well. Many people have prior experience owing something at least in that ballpark. Maybe a $20,000 car loan, or $200,000 home mortgage, etc.

So using relativity, the national debt is no longer just an emotional reaction. We have succeeded in changing that $19 trillion number into something we can relate to.

OK, you owe $150,000. You didn't think much about it, but your government did it for you. You paid them to do it. In theory, they did it because it was in your best interests. Did they do good or bad? That decision is your own to make.

What is your return on that investment? Only you can decide the value of what you got from the government in exchange for what you paid in plus the $150,000 you still owe. But the first step for everyone is making the number into something you can relate to objectively.

For me, $19 trillion "sounded" too big. In fact, a certain cohort wants you to "feel" it's hopeless and impossible to pay off. But $150,000 per adult is manageable. Instead of a home mortgage, or just by adding about $600 per month to your existing mortgage payment, you get to pay off the debt.

Definitely not a happy thought, but it's far from impossible. Making that $19 trillion number into something we can all relate to makes it easy to comprehend. It makes it possible to have a discussion based on critical thinking.

Instead of stupid emotional debates, wouldn't it be better if everyone just discussed how to handle their $150,000 debt? How about tacking $150,000 on to every home mortgage? Is that a bad solution? Maybe... maybe not... either way, it illustrates how you make an emotional problem into something people can discuss objectively.

Critical thinking can solve problems like this pretty quickly. But emotional debates go on for as long as the emotion can be sustained.

With a little more critical thinking, we'd decide it's best for a country to deal with debt while it's still manageable. *Learn from History.* The austerity after a default is far worse than the belt-tightening needed to pay off the debt. And *Trust Common Sense.* No one really believes it's possible to spend more than you take in. They're just hearing what they want to hear. *Follow the Money.* Someone else is putting money in their pockets.

Everyone will pay the bill, sooner or later, but the

critical thinkers will be way out ahead in protecting themselves and profiting.

We use relativity to make ideas or concepts into something clearer and easier for everyone to relate to. Everyone starts from a common reference point. Now we can continue talking about Star Trek and Seinfeld, or the $150,000 we all owe, and we're all discussing the same thing.

Relativity is an advanced way to help *Define the Target*.

11.
Really Respect Nature

NATURE FUNCTIONS WITHOUT our input. The universe is vast, unaware of our existence, and nature is violent. Stars explode, meteors collide, lightning strikes, and never once does the universe worry about humans. We need nature, nature does not need us. In fact, there's considerable evidence nature is better off without us. Maybe we should think about that a little.

Old critical thinker's joke (stop me if you've heard this one.) Two physicists are working in a lab.

Number one: I've just proven the world is going to explode in a million years.

Number two: A million years?

Number one: Sorry, I meant a billion years.

Number two; Phew! For a minute there you had me worried.

Respect Nature is useful on its own as a basic principle. But its real power in guiding us to the best answers comes from giving us the right point of view. We don't always "know our place", but nature always defines our place very well. Objectively. When we distort it too much, nature forces us back into reality. Nature will be here long after all physicists are dead.

Everything we see, we see from our point of view.

Define the Target. Point of View – the position from which something is observed. Point of view always influences what you see. But it never changes whatever is being observed.

Nature doesn't care about our point of view. When challenged, it will remind us of what is objectively real. For example, if our ego starts to get in the way of critical thinking, we can use nature to put us back in our place. We're just a little piece of a vast universe. Figuring out how we can best function is our own personal challenge. The universe does not change to accommodate us.

Galileo proved the earth revolves around the sun almost 600 years ago. Yet today humans still approach most questions as though we are at the center of the universe. Almost everything we try to explain, we try to explain within the boundaries of a human point of view. The idea something exists without us being the reason is generally ignored.

Side Note: if you want to have some fun at a boring gathering, mention the latest news you just read about the universe. Advances in telescope technology have allowed us to assemble some huge and stunning pictures of the universe. What we've learned from all these huge batches of data about deep space is that everything seems to be radiating outward from our galaxy. The evidence suggests our sun was the first one, and the expanding universe has our sun and earth complex as its nexus.

Now pick whoever is nodding their head the most and say "you read the same thing?" They'll take over for a while. When conversation lags, add "Statistically it's likely another earthlike planet exists out there, and it will be thousands of years behind us in development. We can help them if we're able to contact them." And you can keep this discussion going until you get bored.

The telescope advances are true, but the rest is complete bullshit of course. But you will be able to keep the conversation going for as long as you want. People will just naturally accept the idea we are at the center of the universe. Add in our superiority over all other life forms out there and you could go on for days.

Please forgive me if that sounded mean. But there is a point. Let's move to a real life example of the same thing. See if you can find any difference between my party conversation and this one.

Our ability to track climate data today is advancing at an exponential rate. More and more the evidence is telling us that the globe is warming. If we don't do something about it soon, we will wreck the planet. There are many things we should do, like renewable energy and better pollution controls, higher mileage and electric cars, etc. We need to get serious about this while there is still time.

Everyone more or less agrees with that, right? There are insane amounts of money spent just so bureaucrats can sit around big tables and argue about it. This issue is becoming a "sacred cow". You will even suffer ridicule in some social circles today if you disagree. An awful lot of people are invested emotionally.

But here's the problem for critical thinkers. It's the same bullshit story as my pictures from space conversation.

Let's apply some critical thinking.

The age of the earth is estimated to be about 4.5 billion years.

Systematic recorded observations of the weather are somewhat common dating back into the 1500's. They are in ship's logs and things like that. People understood rainy seasons and similar patterns, but they're not very precise. They indicate people were tracking the weather, but the actual data is not really useful.

Galileo is credited with inventing the first device to actually measure temperature on a numbered scale, back around the turn of the Century 1600. It makes a great gift today and is accurate to within about 5 degrees F. That was an amazing achievement for the time. *Learn from History*. Anytime you hear Galileo's name mentioned, it's probably a good idea to consider what he said. Galileo is a giant among critical thinkers.

The USA national weather service began officially tracking the weather in 1870. The UK believes their data reliable from about 1914 onward.

Critical thinking problem number one: nature has been around a lot longer than we've been observing it. Billions of years of weather and only a few hundred years observing it. We don't have enough years of data for any comparison to be statistically significant.

Side note: let's acknowledge there are creationists in the audience. Most believe the Earth to be between 6,000 and 12,000 years old. Still a problem for our statistics. Having data for the most recent 1 percent of that time is still not statistically significant either. And this serves to illustrate even more just how insignificant the data is if you believe Earth is billions of years old.

That's really enough right there for a critical thinker. I have better uses for my time. But let's continue to practice critical thinking and further make the point. *Open Mind* is required for more. This next part makes it more relevant to today, and this same technique can be applied to evaluating many "scientific" observations.

In 1960 the average brand new thermometer was considered accurate within 5%. Accuracy worsens further with age. Later versions started out accurate to 2% and with less deterioration. All of these are read with the naked eye.

There's more. Placement of the measuring devices has changed. The observation points and the surrounding influences have changed. And the devices we use today have changed. None of these variables used to gather the data has been constant over the years generating the data.

So accuracy is at best a plus or minus 5%? (That's being generous. I could convincingly argue the variance is 10%.)

The consensus estimate is we've increased the global temperature roughly 1-degree C over the last 100 years. Some say a little less, and some say a little more. But nobody is claiming 5 degrees or anywhere close to it.

So bottom line, there is no objective mathematical way to support a claim of humans causing global warming.

You can only take an irrelevantly small set of data, define it as the whole, and then find significance in the variance. And you have to do it all while ignoring the effect of changes in how that data was collected.

A critical thinker can only draw one conclusion. This is just selling with bad statistics. *Follow the Money.* Who is gaining from this story? We're not exploring that path here; this is not a political stance. And both sides of the argument have substantial investments in their positions at this point so neither is being 100% honest. But now that you're a critical thinker, don't let anyone profit at your expense over this issue.

For many people, the first reaction will be hating this example. It's a sacred cow and people are emotionally invested. How can saving the planet be wrong! Well, I'm sorry about that. We're here to think critically, not emotionally. And if you want to keep believing anyway, that's ok too. Just be enough of a critical thinker to admit it's an emotional belief. You feel better believing it.

And feeling better really is a good enough reason to think something, if that's your goal. If any purely objective conclusion makes you too unhappy, then sometimes it's better to consider ignoring it, at least until you can reconcile objectivity with emotions. Being unhappy is not the goal of critical thinking. We all hang on to some emotional beliefs. We are all trying to feel good most of the time. But we stand a better chance at long-term success if our decisions are based on reality.

To be clear, personally I think only stupid people disrespect their habitat. But I think that for a critical thinking reason, and not because I think it matters to the planet. *Respect Nature.* I am not the center of the universe. I'm a tiny piece of it. And the planet will be fine with or without humans. Wouldn't it be a more honest discussion if we talked about saving ourselves? The planet doesn't need saving. It will be here long after humans are gone.

And on the specific subject of climate change, there is plenty of objective evidence showing previous ice ages and global warming cycles on Earth. The cycles are much longer than a human lifespan, and they continue whether or not we're here measuring them. It is the ultimate in hubris to insist that climate change be explained on human terms in the space of a few lifetimes or that humans can do anything about it. The cycles take thousands of years. Nature's cycles are not timed to match a human lifespan. *First Things First.* Just accept it and spend the time thinking about something that makes your life better.

Respect Nature. Any critical thinking about your place in the universe demands that you be humble. We're riding along where ever nature wants to go. And only a stupid person spits into the wind.

12.
Mirroring

DEFINE THE TARGET. Mirroring - the behavior in which one person subconsciously imitates the gesture, speech pattern, or attitude of another or group of others.

Most dictionary definitions include the concept of "subconsciously", meaning doing it without thinking about it. And that is true most of the time. Mirroring often occurs in social situations, particularly in the company of close friends or family.

But frequently mirroring is used with full knowledge and intent in order to manipulate you into doing something. Either way, it's behavior where you are acting without thinking. Someone else is making the decisions for you.

Don't Be Distracted and *Think for Yourself*. Both of these principles are required to critically think through a mirroring situation.

Humans mirror naturally; it's a survival instinct, and usually it's just something natural. The problem starts when certain people use it to get a decision from you that critical thinking would prevent.

An easy example would be comedians are always funnier in a room full of people. You are happier if everyone around you is happy. You laugh more if everyone around you is laughing. Laughing at a comedian is usually harmless. So you can be aware of this mirroring and still let it happen.

There is a perfectly illustrative scene in the movie "Annie Hall" where two former writing partners are discussing the laugh track being added to a TV show. Both acknowledge the show is not funny, and the debate is over the morality of manipulating the audience.

What's poignant about that example is the movie is 40 years old. And the people writing it were aware enough of mirroring as a manipulation tool that you could put a whole scene in a movie to debate its morality. (And the scene really was funny too. Without a laugh track added.)

Today, mirroring is used all the time and people just follow along like an obedient herd.

Laughing is appropriate in many circumstances. If you're in an audience at a comedy club, you don't have to think too much. You're there to laugh and whatever the manipulation being used is probably OK. But it doesn't hurt to know the audience is seeded with people to help you laugh. You might analyze the jokes more critically.

But laughing can also be the wrong answer. When you find yourself in a crowd laughing at a message that someone else is taking seriously, some critical thinking is required. The speaker is serious. Why are people laughing? Skillful manipulators will always try to overwhelm a truth by getting the masses to laugh at it.

Learn from History. Early reactions to the claim germs existed were handled this way. So were suggestions the earth was round. The early scientists were ridiculed. We can all think of more modern examples of that same concept.

Be very careful when everyone is laughing and you're not sure something is funny. We don't have the perspective of history to know what's funny and what's true with current events. And you don't want to be a stupid mirror.

Passions of all kinds run stronger when fueled by the people around you. Comedy as we already discussed. Dance floors are either crowded or empty. Food tastes better when shared. But as the emotions grow more serious, the critical thinking needs to be stepped up as well. You really don't want to be angry just because you're mirroring.

Whenever you see a politician with people behind them all looking the same way, you are looking into a mirror and expected to also act the same way. Immediately your critical thinking alarm has to go off and you resist the behavior while analyzing the question.

On an individual level, you will encounter mirroring when dealing with a skilled sales person. They will make you feel very comfortable by mirroring you. They will adopt similar posture, speech patterns, sense of humor, etc. A good salesperson will have you feeling that he is just like you. When you notice that, stop and be sure to evaluate your purchase critically.

In all cases, you do not want to make any important

decisions in this herd mindset. It's ok to laugh along with everyone at a comedian, but you sure don't want to buy a house the same way. Or go on strike that way. Or go to war that way.

Media is so pervasive in our lives today that manipulation is everywhere. If you defend against mirroring enough, you might start to feel a little paranoid. But always remember, it's not paranoia if it's real. And smart people are using mirroring on you every day.

Rejecting it becomes automatic for a critical thinker. It's not a big deal once you make it a habit. But like we keep saying, you have to really do it. Just understanding mirroring will not prevent it.

And by the way, you can use mirroring to your advantage once you understand it. But we'll save that for a book on communication techniques.

13.
Follow the Money Deeper

EVERYONE HAS THOUGHT of *Follow the Money* before as a concept. In obvious situations, everyone is on guard against it. The simple example would be the stereotypical used car salesman. You just assume they'll say anything to get your money.

But do you really *Follow the Money* using critical thinking? When you see an ad for a drug that says it's 75% effective, you know they are trying to sell you the drug. But do you *Follow the Money* all the way through that 75% claim too? Let's hope so. That's basic critical thinking and we covered it in the first book.

Now let's advance it. And again, this example is chosen to challenge critical thinking with emotion. Advanced critical thinking must reach objective conclusions.

Elsewhere in this book we analyze the Zika virus and critically think about its prominence on the international stage. And let's all agree up front, mosquito-borne illnesses really are a terrible thing. But if you *Follow the Money*, you find more people benefitting from fighting the Zika fight than there are actual victims suffering from the disease. There's a lot of bad decision-making going on.

Whenever you see a stampede to throw money at a problem, *Follow the Money* and not the problem.

To *Follow the Money* on Zika deeper, let's look at the 2016 Summer Olympics. They were in Rio de Janeiro, from August 5th through the 21st. It's also peak Zika-frenzy time.

Now unless you've been living under a rock, you're aware the Olympics has degraded itself into primarily a political competition with enormous sums of money at stake. The 2012 summer Olympics cost London an estimated 15 billion pounds. And by all accounts, they turned a profit. Beyond the economics specific to the event, there are other financial gains that outweigh and outlast the event itself.

Sochi (Russia) claims to have spent $50 billion for their Olympics. And Beijing $40 billion in 2008. Vancouver got off cheap in 2010 at $7 billion. To make all that into something we can all relate to, if the Olympics were an S&P 500 company, they would rank about 195 by revenue. They are bigger than Occidental Petroleum, Visa, E-Bay, Campbell's Soup and many other big names you know. Bottom line, the Olympics is big business being played out at the highest levels.

Zika virus is a bad thing, as we all agreed. But a critical thinker cannot help but observe Brazil has always had a high incidence of mosquito-borne disease. In fact, the total number of Zika cases is statistically insignificant. When included with Brazil's overall mosquito disease problems, the incidence of Zika is not even a worthy footnote.

Over the past five years, millions of people have been infected with diseases transmitted by mosquitos in Brazil. Millions.

Total Zika cases reported in Brazil as we write this? About 7,000. That's right, all the news mania you've been hearing, athletes skipping the games etc., it's all based on about 7,000 cases. And we're willing to bet half of those are really Dengue fever anyway. Dengue has been around a long time, it hits millions of people, but it's impossible to whip people into a frenzy over it anymore. No one will throw more money at Dengue. Right now, whenever possible, you'd rather call it Zika virus.

Follow the Money. Who gains and who loses by Brazil's Olympics being devalued over this "new" health emergency? We'll leave you to work that one out for yourself. Our point here is to illustrate following the money deeper.

When there's money being thrown at a problem, always *Follow the Money.* The problem is usually just a distraction.

14.
Interlude: Bad Decision #1

SPINAL FUSION IS a surgery that used to be very common. The fundamental idea was to stop movement in the area of the spine causing pain. There was a major surge in the use of the procedure in 1990's into early 2000's. It is a major surgery, lasting hours and having a long recovery period. At its peak, it was roughly a $40 billion industry.

One problem for a critical thinker. There was never any data supporting the theory. From some points of view it sounded reasonable, but there was no data. People in pain trusted instead of thinking, and it grew into a $40 billion industry.

In 2011, Blue Cross stopped paying for spinal fusion for the most common recommendations like degenerative discs, etc. Well-controlled studies had been conducted. And after a comprehensive review of data, there was no difference between patients having the surgery and patients having no surgery. And there were better results among those who did physical therapy instead of surgery. In other words, a major surgery with full anesthesia and possibilities of complications is worse for you than just getting a little exercise.

Today all insurers make it much harder to qualify

spinal fusion surgeries for reimbursement. (Irony? A financial decision by insurance companies that's good for people.)

Yet the impassioned arguments trying to get this surgery paid for continue. Insurance companies are bad, getting between doctor and patient, etc. No data, just emotional arguments to pay for a discredited treatment.

All of this makes perfect sense to a critical thinker. Severe back pain affects a staggering 80% of people at some time in their life. That's a lot of customers! Time for our *Common Sense* alarm bell to sound. The following line of thinking is automatic whenever you're making a decision like this:

Follow the Money. The profit to the providers is huge.

Think for Yourself. Being the "indicated treatment" or "standard of care" does not make it a good decision. It just means the herd is doing it. And the herd is wrong way too often to be trusted.

Respect Nature. The spine is designed to be very flexible, and rotate too. Fusing it so it cannot move sounds like the opposite of what nature intended.

And finally *There Will Be Math.* Review the data. No data? Then it's just bullshit.

Like 80% of people, I have personal experience with severe back pain. Surgery sounded stupid to me. Exercise is a daily habit and I do Pilates two or three times a week. No anesthesia required. And I am pain-free about 99% of the time. Actually, sitting and writing is about the worst thing I do for my back...

There is a proverb common to many different cultures saying essentially this: "You are only as young as your spine is flexible."

I will add it's a sad day for critical thinking when we need insurance companies to protect us from the medical industry. *Think for Yourself*.

15.
Words, Labels and Don't Be Distracted

DISTRACTION IS ONE of the most practiced skills in the world. Most attempts to control your behavior use distractions to dull your critical thinking process. Advertising is the most obvious offender, and we explored that in Book One. Just de-programming yourself from advertising will seriously advance the quality of your decisions.

Now let's advance it up another level.

Names are used to cause confusion and direct people to a different line of thought. Let's use a simple example. You probably know this one already. We have a product named 2% milk. Sounds good. Any food with only 2% fat content is probably a good thing. But the fat content of whole milk is only around 3.25%. The difference is about 20 calories in an 8 oz. glass.

But even when you know the numbers, "whole milk" still sounds a lot fatter than "2%". That's the power of programming. And if you believe whole milk is healthier, it also becomes a counter-intuitive decision.

Now let's move to an example more worthy of advanced critical thinking. We addressed this before, but this one is important and we'll come at it from a different critical thinking direction this time.

The term 401K refers to the section of the tax code making it possible for this type of financial account to defer taxes. To market a 401K, to sell it to you, it is called "saving for retirement". Who can argue with such a worthy goal? But "saving" really means something else entirely. Putting money in your 401K means betting that stocks and bonds will improve in value. That's also called "playing the market". All you gain with a 401K is the tax deferral.

Why don't we call it "playing the market with deferred taxes"?

The name change to "saving for retirement" makes it sound like a much more noble pursuit. It's much easier to sell you that way. Now let's restate it more honestly:

"Give me 10% of your paycheck for the next 30 years. I will buy and sell different types of business assets with your money. I am very limited in the scope of what I can buy. I must choose between stocks or bonds and their derivatives, issued by relatively large businesses or governments. I will try my best to make a profit. You will pay all the expenses associated with the transactions. You will also pay my fee each year regardless of whether or not I make a profit. When you reach retirement age, you will get back the final result of all this activity."

That's an honest critical thinking statement of the 401K proposition and mainstream "saving for retirement" advice you hear everywhere today. It sounds like a lousy proposition when stated honestly. (Don't blame me. It wasn't my idea; I'm just thinking about it.)

The world of possibilities for your investable funds is much larger than the overpriced stocks and bonds offered by bankrupt governments and bloated businesses. Who pays 15 times earnings to buy a company? Or lends money for 10 years at 2 or 3% interest? No one in the private sector, that's for sure. But it's business as usual in the public markets. Where do the buyers come from? That would be the 401k accounts, along with any other way the sellers can sucker the public into "investing" in these overpriced assets. *Don't Be Distracted*. You can "play the markets" and might even win a little, but it's not "saving". It's gambling.

If you want to know more about investing, read our book on it. The point here is to illustrate how naming this concept "saving for retirement" changes a 401K into something that sounds completely different from what it really is. A critical thinker has to analyze past the names and understand what's real. After enough time, it all just becomes 2% milk. Unless your brain is trained to critical thinking, you just react however they want.

Name calling also is used to make an idea sound worse. Watch how often someone insults someone else when they don't like what they're saying. Someone probably called my restatement of the 401K proposition "stupid". *Don't Be Distracted* by insults. An objective statement is unchanged by name calling or any other emotional attachment. Back in the dark ages, this was taught as the logical fallacy "ad hominem", meaning addressing argument toward the messenger instead of the message. In the common tongue, Don't Shoot the

Messenger!

Another standard distraction technique is to state facts no one can disagree with, and then attach something being sold or promoted. Most often this manifests as the "any answer is the right answer" fallacy. The problem is bad, everyone agrees, and therefore the attached solution must be a good idea.

Analyzing real world examples of this requires a commitment to critical thinking. The problems are real, and sometimes terrible. Emotions run strong. You start out feeling like you just have to do something about it. And fast too.

But to do any good, you have to be able to distinguish between the real problem and a proposed solution. The real problem is objective, a statement of fact that is required for the critical thinking process. The proposed solution is just a proposal. It's just an idea. You need some data to decide if it's a good idea or not.

For our example here, let's use the TSA. Everyone agrees terrorists crashing airplanes is an unacceptable problem. The solution put into effect is the Transportation Safety Administration. Hold onto that idea for a minute, we'll come back to it.

A variation on the distraction of using well-understood facts is the "after this, therefore because of this" method. It's terribly flawed logic, but still used all the time with great effectiveness. Once you get accustomed to spotting this distraction, you will be amazed and annoyed at how often it works.

Here's a silly example to make the point: "I had chicken for dinner last night and it's raining this morning, therefore my chicken dinner caused the rain."

That was ridiculous to make it clear. Now let's try this one: "The TSA has been removing passenger's shoes for the last several years. We've had no terrorists shoe bomb an American airplane. Therefore, the TSA surveillance worked." Yeah, right.

Let's use the birth and implementation of the Transportation Safety Administration as our advanced concepts example for *Don't Be Distracted*. They gave it a great name, claimed it was the solution to a problem we all know is terrible, and claim the results are the proof it's working.

Where is the critical thinking in all that? Let's just pick a point and jump in.

There have been numerous studies and tests showing the TSA is very bad at stopping weapons and bombs from getting on planes. No terrorists, thankfully, but "test" teams succeed in getting past security a staggeringly high percentage of the time. In one well-published test, they succeeded in 67 out of 70 attempts to smuggle weapons on to a plane. Meanwhile. The TSA confiscated the water bottle you forgot was in your pack. And didn't even smile at you courteously.

Conclusion: maybe there's another reason no one has successfully hijacked a plane recently?

Let's dig further. *Follow the Money*. The TSA has a budget of $8 billion and employs about 60,000 people. Most of that cost eventually ends up in your airline ticket, although some is paid by the general revenue fund including taxes from people who never fly. So bottom line, a terrible crisis resulted in the creation of yet another bureaucracy that does its job poorly.

Dig further. Other countries do it better and cheaper. Israel is the "gold standard" for airline security. They still use old-fashioned metal detectors, passengers keep their shoes on, and you can usually take your food with you too.

Don't Be Distracted. To a critical thinker, TSA surveillance sounds just like the chicken dinner. And the bigger problem is the cost a society is willing to accept due to this lack of critical thinking. Taking your shoes off may not bother you, but add up all the time people spend standing in line, the abuses, the cost of lawsuits, and... eventually you get to a very large amount of expense tied to a program of questionable value.

We'll stop that example here. This is not meant to be a political rant. The point is to illustrate what happens when the lack of critical thinking is institutionalized. We all pay the price.

Let's switch gears to some common but less contentious examples.

Define the Target. Entertainment – Providing amusement or enjoyment. Entertainment is not about facts, and it's not about critical thinking. Anyone who thinks the size of an audience correlates with expertise... well, that's just stupid.

Entertainment is used to sell more serious ideas. Ideas that should use critical thinking instead. Let's analyze one. We'll use a genre here in order to avoid offending any fans of individual programs.

A whole school of "reality" programming has sprung up around the idea of "inspired by true events". It's become the same thing as a documentary, even though the producers are careful to warn everyone in advance that it's only inspired by true events.

That means it's a story. Fiction, inspired by true events. Like the movie Titanic. Yes, the boat really sank, but Leo DiCaprio was not on the boat, and no rich old ladies lost any giant blue diamond necklaces. Great movie, inspired by true events.

Like I said, I don't want to make enemies by naming current movies or TV programs, But I think we can use Michael Moore as an easy reference here. He freely admits his movies have a "point of view" and may slant the presentation of the facts a little. We'll add, he slants a lot more than just a little, but we still enjoy his work.

In any case, *Don't Be Distracted*. Critical thinkers don't get their facts from entertainment.

16.
There Will Be a Lot More Math

THE WORLD IS a mathematical place. It has to be, because math was developed by humans to explain the world. Math is a universal language. And you have to speak it well enough to make good decisions.

There Will Be Math is likely the most challenging of our critical thinking principles. It is possible to be a good critical thinker and avoid most math. But to be a great critical thinker, you have to step up and run some numbers. Don't worry, we'll stop before doing any calculus. But we should at least be aware of factorials because many bad decisions have a ripple effect that multiplies the effect of the mistake.

We're not going to enter the academic debate over defining "what is mathematics". We'll leave that to professors trying to convince students to take their classes. Instead, we will *Simplify*. Math has no purpose unless it's being used to explain something else. There is no point to any formula or number or combination or iteration unless the result helps explain something else in the real world.

And a little math can be a HUGE benefit in explaining things. But the people using it have to speak the language. If you cannot do some math, then the communication is no better than someone giving you directions in a foreign language you do not understand. Speaking "a little math" is no better than speaking "a little Mandarin". You will still find yourself lost on the way to the bathroom.

To be a great critical thinker, you have to apply some math to the world around you, and you must recognize bad math when you see it. We really could not care less about people studying calculus or the professor's empty classroom. But we are very concerned at how much bad math is readily accepted today because the people hearing it don't know any better.

In most cases, the most efficient first step of critical thinking is to do some math. Whenever math can be used, the results tend to be certain. People lie, numbers do not. Of course, people do distort numbers all the time trying to make them lie. But critical thinkers can work their way through the bullshit because critical thinkers do the math. We don't just accept the numbers or explanations that other people tell us.

This chapter will be divided into subtopics:

Return on Investment. The concept of ROI is routinely applied to investments. Even in that simplest of applications, people usually get it wrong. *Define the Target*. ROI is what you get back in exchange for what you put in. Simple ROI example: I loan you $100 and you pay me back $105. My ROI is $5 or 5% of my investment.

Now let's make it more abstract. More "advanced concept" worthy. I washed my car by hand this morning. My investment looks pretty easy to define: my time, energy and the cost of materials used. And my ROI is the clean car. Sound correct? Not really, it's just the beginning. My investment also includes the opportunity cost of anything else I could have done with that time or money. For example, would my wife have been happier if I took her to breakfast instead? Now my car washing investment includes a less happy wife.

What about the ROI on my car washing investment? This is where a critical thinker regularly and routinely makes their life better than most. The clean car is not the return on investment. It's just a clean car. It has no empirical value. So what is my return on investment? Why did I do it?

I can't answer that. I would never wash a car if my wife would rather go to breakfast. Really, I'd only wash a car if I had absolutely nothing else to do and wanted the exercise. There's almost always something offering me a better ROI. Most people wash cars because they just accept some empirical value to a clean car. A lot of people are even regulars at a car wash where they pay someone else to do it for them. Do they all value a clean car that highly? I doubt it. Someone else put that idea in their head and they just accepted it.

The point is no result is ever your return on investment. It's just the answer to an equation. And the answer to any math problem is worthless unless it explains something else. *Think for Yourself*. Whatever the result of your effort, don't just accept it as good. Start by saying "So what?". Keep asking until the answer means something to you. That answer is your return on investment.

When you start thinking about your own personal ROI whenever you expend some effort or assets, it changes many of your actions. The value of way too much in the world has been programmed into us by external forces. A critical thinker does not just accept it. What do we really get for that investment?

Apply ROI in real life. Is your paycheck the return on your work investment? Of course not. What do you buy with that paycheck? Now you're getting closer. You buy a lot of things. You have to look at the value of each of them. Some of them, maybe a lot of them, you just accept the value someone else put on them. Like the clean car. So you have to take those another step, or as many steps as required to find the real and empirical value to yourself. When you get to the end of that analysis, now you have a direct critical thinking link between your investment in work and your return on that investment.

Right about now a whole bunch of people are saying that's way too hard. And yes, we agree. It is way too hard if you jump in and start right there. But this is the Advanced Concepts book. If you're already automatic in applying the basic critical thinking principles, now you're just layering the ROI concept on top of it. Easy. Well, at least not unreasonably difficult.

In any case, you should have already done some critical thinking about your budget. We're just connecting with what you invested so you can evaluate the decisions even more critically. When you directly make a connection between effort expended and the value you get in return, it changes many budget decisions. If you see the expensive wine as three hours work in a bottle, you will spend less on wine. Guaranteed.

Let's *Simplify*. For any investment, know your real return. Really understand how much you value what comes back to you in return for what you put in.

A critical thinker might *Think for Themselves* and decide washing the car will make them really happy. That's OK too, if they really understand why.

Diminishing Returns. OK, if we're good with ROI we can progress to the more advanced concept of Diminishing Returns. *Define the Target*. Diminishing Returns means each repetition of an investment yields progressively less return.

Simple example. We just washed our car. We can wash it again and it will be cleaner, but less dirt will be removed with the second washing. Then we wash it a third time. There will still be some additional dirt removed, but the change will be even less than the second cleaning. And you can continue this progression until the change from additional investment is so small it cannot even be measured.

As with all our simple examples, it should look easy and the principle almost looks too simple. Now let's use it. Because you are probably allowing Diminishing Returns too far into your life every day. We will list some quick examples:

You get substantially the same results by using half the recommended quantity of many products: laundry detergents, toothpaste, mouthwash, vitamins and nutrition supplements and many more. In all cases, it pays to critically think about the seller's recommended amount. *Follow the Money.* The more you use the more they sell. Do you expect them to recommend the minimum that works or the maximum they can get away with? Your clothes might be a little cleaner using a full cup of detergent, but they won't be twice as clean as when using half-a-cup.

Another good example is salt. Some salt is necessary in many foods. Unsalted bread tastes pretty bad. Let's say you're making a loaf using 4 cups or roughly 500 grams of flour. No salt and nobody will eat it. Now add salt. Starting at about 3 grams of salt most of the bread will get eaten without comment. Keep adding a gram at a time and it will keep getting better, but the difference with each addition will not be as dramatic as the previous one. You will reach an optimal amount for your taste, but the return from each addition will diminish.

If you need to cut sodium in your diet, reversing this approach works very well. Just diminish salt one gram at a time until you notice your enjoyment suffering too much.

Now let's advance Diminishing Returns in our daily life just a little more. We just took our wife to breakfast (instead of washing the car) and it made her very happy. Now we're thinking about lunch. Taking her out to lunch would make her happy too, but not as happy as breakfast. Then there is dinner. There is a good chance if we take her out to dinner too, it will not make her much happier at all. Thinking about Diminishing Returns has a place in all your relationships.

Diminishing Returns can actually turn negative. If we

take our wife out to eat too often, she might even get tired of restaurant food. "Too much of a good thing".

Simple example: Feeding the birds once seems nice and they might appreciate a day off from worm hunting. Feed them every day and they will expect it, not appreciate it, feed them too long and they will forget how to feed themselves. At that point, they will die if you do not feed them. Diminishing Returns took them from a vacation day to death.

With virtually all investments, there is a Diminishing Returns curve. There is always an optimal investment in any given set of circumstances. The critical thinker is seeking that point. And everyone else profits off your investments to the extent you are incorrect in finding that optimal point.

Used together, Return on Investment and Diminishing Returns are powerful critical thinking tools. By combining them, a critical thinker optimizes how they spend their life. *Time is Precious*. You want to invest time optimally.

Our math chapter is getting long. Sorry. We knew that would happen and kind of warned you at the start. But we cannot leave without discussing bad statistics.

Bad Statistics.

By the way, you notice how medical problems are getting catchy marketing names? RA, RLS, ASPS, Adult ADHD, Low-T. That's to grab your attention so you can buy their cures. We want to do something like that with the bad statistics they use to sell all the drugs for those catchy names. Bad Stats. It's a disease too. BS.

Define the Target. Statistics. The practice of analyzing a set of data for the purpose of inferring proportion in the whole from a smaller sample of that whole. In the common tongue, you collect data until you have enough to predict what you will get if you continue collecting. The degree of accuracy in your predictions is what proves whether or not you have good statistics.

You can try to identify patterns in any set of data. If the set is large enough, you will always find something, even if the data is truly random. But, if you cannot reliably predict when it will repeat, then drawing any conclusion is just bad statistics. BS.

In today's world, virtually everything being sold uses bad statistics somehow. Even if they just tell you your teeth are 22% whiter. We will spare you from too many calculations. But you must be aware of the concepts so you can include them in your critical thinking decisions.

Analysis can be done on any amount of data, large or small. Any set of data can be turned into statistics. And you can make predictions based on any amount of data. But only the accuracy of those predictions matters to a critical thinker.

When someone gives you a statistic, your first reaction has to be "how accurate is that?". Who did the analysis? Was the data set relevant? Was the data truly random? Was the study double-blind? (Double-blind is the "gold standard" for scientific proofs.) Your ultimate question is: how much is this data worth in my decision?

If the statistics you evaluate come from a double-blind

study and in sufficient quantity to be statistically significant, then it probably deserves a lot of weight in your decision. And if the statistics come from anything else, you must immediately start discounting the claim. That is not to say the claims are always false, but the more the numbers are stretched to reach a conclusion, the more suspect you have to be. Especially if that conclusion includes you paying for something.

Many products, most frequently drugs, are sold after getting the minimum amount of data required to make a statistic sound reliable. Not mathematically reliable, just enough math to make a good sales pitch. And unfortunately, the people doing the evaluations are not always critical thinkers. Many billions in drugs are sold every year based on stunningly bad statistics.

We will look at one drug example, statins, later in the book. But perhaps health care more than anywhere else is where people really need critical thinking and *There Will Be Math*. Prescription drugs are powerful, they change what your body does, you take them every day, and most people would be stunned at the limited data driving all those prescriptions.

And that helps us make our final point for this chapter on *There Will Be Math*. People lie, numbers do not. Math is a critical thinkers best friend, and it stops stupidity fast.

17.
Rationalizations

RATIONALIZATIONS ARE JUST people spending their time trying to believe something they want to be true but have not yet proven objectively. It's a combined violation of *Open Mind* and *Don't Be Distracted*. You won't find the right answer if you're already working hard to believe something else.

Smart people are their own worst enemy. When talking to yourself, you can be either the easiest to bullshit or the most difficult. On different days, you are likely both. Once you're a critical thinker, bullshitting yourself becomes impossible.

It starts with being on guard against hearing what you want to hear. *Don't Be Distracted*. Theories are not fact no matter how rational they sound or how eloquently they are stated. You can enjoy someone's command of language, but still not accept the ideas being proposed. Two things can be true. Someone can sound great and still be wrong.

Great speakers stir up strong emotions. That skill can be used for good or evil. Either way, emotions are not part of critical thinking. Great speakers can be enjoyed for their talent, the same way you might enjoy a symphony orchestra. Or Beyonce... oops, there we go again. *Don't Be Distracted*. But if the band leader turns around and starts talking politics, he's no different from anyone else in the room. The skill at manipulating emotions does not make any critical thinking difference.

Persuasive use of language can be found in "science" all the time. And many fallacies hide under the banner of "science". People get very passionate about theories they want to be true. In many cases, theories are built on other theories, and if one turns out to be false, then the whole house comes tumbling down.

In fact, the deeper the theory goes, the more likely there will be some serious rationalizations going on as it falls apart.

Imagine the first time someone figured out leeches weren't working. There was all that history and useless leeching-gear physicians had to deal with… no doubt a lot of rationalizing went on for a while.

Or move the example to something more recent. About 60 years ago, more doctors recommended Camel cigarettes than any other brand. Doctors were used for years as the advertising answer to mounting evidence that smoking was bad for you. It's pretty easy to rationalize your smoking if the doctors are choosing the same brand.

Let's move the example to today. Apply critical thinking to everything you hear about high fructose corn syrup (HFC).

There Will Be Math. Start in the year 1960 and overlay a graph of obesity in the USA with the introduction of HFC. Widespread use of HFC started around 1970. Now do the same thing with HFC and ADHD. I'm trying to illustrate critical thinking, not take a firm position on HFC here. But I will say that all the scientists saying HFC is the same as any other sugar sound pretty much the same as doctors recommending camels. Always *Follow the Money*.

There Will Be Math. If you're a big investor in Cargill or Archer Daniels Midland, then you really want to believe HFC is great stuff. *Open Mind*. Critical thinking doesn't care one way or the other. No rationalizing, only facts.

Without supporting data, science is just people thinking out loud. They tend to be people who sound like they know something. And if they're saying what people want to hear, then people work very hard to believe them. Our favorite example of this is Spontaneous Generation.

Define the Target. Spontaneous Generation – The production of living organisms from non-living matter. For example, there was a time when maggots were thought to just come from meat.

Learn from History. Spontaneous Generation was still widely accepted as scientific fact less than 300 years ago. Experiments disproving the theory began as early as the 1660's but people's unwillingness to believe in life they could not see, their lack of an *Open Mind*, led them to accept rationalizations instead of facts.

Eventually, enough hard data from repeatable testing made it impossible to prove spontaneous generation was real. So this scientific "fact" was proven false and it was largely abandoned by the mid-1800's. But that was 200 years after data started proving it was false.

Let's *Learn from History*. Can we apply anything learned about Spontaneous Generation to today? Try to imagine all the time wasted and brain space spent by truly intelligent people trying to hang on to this disproven theory. Now apply it to people trying to hang on to something without proof today. Maybe the belief that a low-cholesterol diet is good for your health? Or that high fructose corn syrup is ok? Or Camel cigarettes are ok?

Learning from History can be very easy because hindsight is perfect. We already know what came later so the results are clear. But at a more advanced level, learning to avoid the mistakes made during that historical learning process can accelerate our learning today.

Many people recognize this Benjamin Franklin quote:

> *"You will observe with concern how long a useful truth may be known and exist before it is generally received and practiced upon."*

Not everyone is aware he was lamenting the fact that the "mischievous" effects of lead poisoning had already been shown for about 60 years and no one was paying attention. Wonder how much Ben would lament over Flint, Michigan today.

We'll leave you with one final example to watch. Tesla is upsetting the car distribution model. There are many places trying to prevent them from selling directly to the public. And many of the arguments center on consumer protections. Follow this and you will be very entertained. Somehow, a certain cohort is convinced that the typical auto dealership protects us from the likes of Tesla. Rationalizations can get absurd.

Avoid rationalizations trying to hang on to old beliefs. Just let the facts come in and don't be afraid to change your mind. Change is necessary to evolve. You get farther faster with an *Open Mind*.

18.
Weird Interlude

As I turned the page last night reading a food magazine, a coupon for Cialis fell out. I'm not really sure what to think about that, but it seems like it fits into a discussion of rationalizations.

Personally, I've never thought about summer squash that way before. But someone in Lilly's advertising department thought it was a good idea for me to think about erections at the same time I'm reading about zucchini bread.

How much rationalizing was done to make that sound like a good idea? How did more than one person agree on it? Imagine the herd mentality in that advertising department... In any case, it failed with me. I found it annoying.

It also made me think less of the magazine, so I won't name it here. But how little respect must they have for their content? Do they really need coupons for unrelated products falling out of the magazine? Revenues that desperate? Critical thinking tip: make your content valuable and you won't need those coupons.

Actually, it was for $200 off the first prescription, though. That's a lot of money. Maybe I should rethink zucchini bread. *Open Mind* and all that...

Big Pharma are the biggest pushers in the drug business. When you see coupons like that, just change whatever their product to heroin. Want a free sample?

19.
Simplify or Rationalize?

OUR *SIMPLIFY* PRINCIPLE was inspired by C.W. Ceram:

> *"Genius is the ability to reduce the complicated to the simple."*

But Confucius gets credit for being the first to say it. Roughly translated, he said, "life is simple until we screw it up".

We like to feel like geniuses. But life is really simple. And people really do screw it up. But at least we know people were doing the same thing back in Confucius' time too. So we have not gone backwards, but we've done such a good job screwing it up that by the time Ceram was writing it takes genius to *Simplify*.

People work very hard to make things more complicated. Complications are always added to advance someone's selfish agenda. They need to impress you, or they want your money or they want you to do something, etc. And if the people adding complications happen to be in a position of power, then the complications usually include attempts to control your decisions.

In "Don't Be Stupid about Critical Thinking" we explored basic examples. So we already know we must be on guard against complications being forced on us by people trying to gain some advantage.

Now for advancing the concept, let's look at the worst way we abuse this principle. It happens when we do it to ourselves. We complicate explanations to ourselves to hide from realities we do not want to accept. Humans go through great mental gyrations trying to avoid admitting some reality they wish was different. That's rationalizing.

We just discussed rationalizing a little earlier. Now let's take a look at it here as a violation of *Simplify*.

Humans use rationalizations to get through life. *Define the Target*. Rationalization – To devise self-satisfying explanations, especially when applied after the fact to making unreasoned thoughts or actions appear reasonable. In other words, we do what we want and then try to make it into a good decision later.

Simple example. You just ate the whole pint of ice cream. When you're finished, you decide your body must have been craving the calcium, and you didn't have any lunch so you must have needed a calorie boost too. And now you've bullshitted yourself into not feeling guilty about it. It would be easier on your brain and good critical thinking to just admit it was great and you lost self-control.

More importantly, if you properly analyze the experience, maybe next time you'd stop at half the pint. Or not. But either way you did not find the right answer. The rationalization puts you in the position of having to do the same mental gymnastics next time. You've made life more complicated.

Rationalizations also violate the *First Things First*

principle. If you want to think efficiently, then don't give yourself the added burden of trying to explain some action after you do it. It is far more efficient to just admit you didn't think about it.

A pint of ice cream isn't so bad, and it makes a good simple example. Now let's make it an advanced example.

The USA went to war in Iraq based on bad intelligence. Today most informed people admit the mistake. The high-ranking public officials of the time all pretty much agree. Some of them have apologized to Colin Powell. But you will still see some elected officials with a certain point of view use really tortured rationalizations to make it OK. If they'd just say "sorry for the mistake" they could move on to solving real problems instead of using up all their brain power for BS.

A critical thinker knows we need people in positions of power that do not engage in rationalizations. When governments repeat these kinds of mistakes, people die. These lessons must be learned if we expect to get something better in the future.

Let's look at one other example with a little less politics attached. This one is dangerous to your wallet instead. New car fever. It happens to most people at one time or another, you've just got to have that new car. And then the rationalizations start pouring in. Better gas mileage, safer for the kids, less likely to break down after dark, better for the environment. On and on, the advertising gives you infinite ways to rationalize your purchase. And then you rationalize leasing instead of buying because, well... the payment is lower so it must be better, right? (if you believe that you better read our money book ASAP.)

Rationalizations are just ways people try to make bad decisions into good ones. As we've discussed elsewhere, if a journey starts in the wrong direction, the only good move is to admit the mistake and start over. As bad decisions pile up, the amount of time wasted on rationalizations makes it impossible to get a great life.

20.
Interlude: Habit #4

LET'S REVISIT OUR word analysis habit one more time.

Word inflation has become a common substitute for facts today. There is so much communication going on, it's difficult for people to stand out. The opportunity to communicate is ubiquitous. And there really isn't that much worth saying.

Most messages are not special. There's just not enough worth saying to fill all the available opportunities. The message doesn't stand out, so the words get inflated.

Everyone's a "hero" now, it's not enough to just be a good person.

People "obsess" now, it's not enough to just be thinking about it.

People are "super" into things, it's not enough to just be interested.

Everyone "survived" something, it's not enough to just overcome a problem.

Word inflation is everywhere if you look for it.

For a critical thinker, inflated words do not make the statements any more powerful. But it does cause us to think about why the speaker is using them.

I want to be a critical thinking hero who's obsessed

with making good decisions and super into making the world a little less stupid.

And if I survive, I'm just using an instinct I have in common with all life forms.

Simplify. Deflate any word inflation to get to the meaningful information.

21.
Learn More from History

LEARN FROM HISTORY. Very often you can see the future by looking into the past.

There are not many questions today that have not been answered before. In Book One, "Don't Be Stupid about Critical Thinking", we looked at this from the perspective of history. All fiat currencies fail, humans are always at war, that sort of thing.

Learn from History is a very important principle and the world would be a much smarter place if people would just pay attention to some of the lessons taught by history. Arguably, the world's greatest thinkers are all dead and part of history now. I think Zuckerberg is a genius, but I don't put Facebook up there with proving the earth is round.

For advancing this principle, we want to look at learning from our own personal history. We don't always have to go back to Confucius to find useful lessons. We can also make better decisions just by learning from our own lives. If we can just manage to avoid repeating our own mistakes, we will have a much better life.

Many of the problems you think about today are just repeats of something that has happened before.

Let's use an example everyone has experienced, either personally or by watching someone else do it. Every year after the holiday season you go on a diet. You choose the most popular diet each year and try it. "Low fat" one year, "low carb" the next, always with the same results. You are deprived of food you like, lose a little weight and then the weight comes back when you stop dieting. So now it's another year, the holidays are over again, and it's time to diet again.

Wait a minute! Now you're a critical thinker. Let's *Learn from History*. I don't enjoy dieting. And diets have never achieved the desired results. Why do it again? Let's do a little analysis this time. If you're 30 lbs. heavier today than you were 10 years ago, then the trend is not good. And dieting is not the answer. Maybe critical thinking is a better option.

First Things First. What is a healthy weight for you? If you were too skinny 10 years ago, maybe things are better now. We need data to *Define the Target*. What is our healthy weight?

OK, after defining the target, maybe the news is bad and we really are 30 lbs. overweight. And we also know that dieting doesn't work. Now what? Critical thinking demands we look at what we've been doing for the last 10 years, and change the behavior causing us to gain weight. *Learn from History*. Experience has shown us changing our diet for a short time does not work. We have to change something else.

Maybe we skip desert and go for a 30-minute walk after dinner each evening. Or maybe just 3 times per week. *There Will Be Math*. Small incremental gains accumulate. It's OK if it takes us a long time, even years, to lose the 30 lbs. we've gained.

Simplify. Our regular lifestyle has to lead to our target weight. And *Think for Yourself.* Your target weight is whatever makes you happiest. It is not what someone else says you should weigh.

Learning from your own history is required to choose a great life. Avoiding previous errors is a benefit that compounds into the future, making more time available for even more valuable decisions.

But don't forget to learn from all the great thinkers that came before us. There really are not many original thoughts today, and if Pythagoras already explored something, I'm going to pay attention to his answers.

Time is Precious. And I could spend the rest of my life trying to figure out something Galileo already answered.

22.
Interlude: Habit #5

COMPARE DECISIONS THAT achieve the same goal. Frequently one includes additional benefits beyond the primary reason for choosing. You can "double-dip", get two returns for one investment.

Double-dipping is part of *There Will Be Math* concept of Return on Investment. You're going to invest the same effort either way, if one choice offers even a remote possibility of extra benefit, it costs nothing extra to get that return.

Simple example, choosing between two routes to a destination. Both routes take nearly the same time. One route has better scenery. You are making the drive, achieving the primary goal of getting to the destination, but if you choose the scenic route you are also enjoying something else along the way. The scenery is your "double-dip".

Also consider alternate choices where one offers only the potential for a double dip. Simple example: You want to get some exercise. You can do it alone in your house, or you can venture out to where you might meet some interesting people. If you're trying to beef up your social calendar, it just makes sense to choose the potential double dip.

Double-dip opportunities come up all the time. You just

have to take the time to watch for them. Too much rushing from one thing to the next prevents the opportunity to see ways to get more out of the same time invested. Eventually you learn going a little slower and choosing all the double-dip opportunities yields more than just rushing through more single purpose choices.

Often, the double dip comes from allowing just a little more time. Instead of automatically choosing the fastest way to get one thing done, you look for more benefit from just a little extra time spent.

You need exercise, need milk, and need to spend some time with your kid. Don't just hop in the car and run to the store because it's fastest. Maybe take a bike ride to the store together. You will get more total value out of the time invested than if you tried to cover all three separately.

And of course, it's always a double-dip if you're considering doing something that would also make your partner happy.

23.
Binary and Forced Choices

YOUR LIFE IS planned out for you before you are born. You don't really have a chance to make any serious choices. We may choose a school or a job, but the choices are limited and the path is the same one as everyone else's. You have a student loan, a mortgage, a car loan, maybe some kids... We have an illusion of freedom, but the whole herd is really headed in the same direction. You only get to choose which part of the same cliff you get to stampede off of.

For example, did you ever have the chance to choose a system where you do not get a job and pay your bills? Did you get to choose to pay taxes? At any time between your birth and today, did you really get to choose your life path freely? You never could have chosen to be a hermit and live off the land or something like that, could you? What about having a harem? OK, here's a more realistic choice: what if you think a Kibbutz is the best life choice?

The answer is invariably "No". All you get to choose is from among a pre-determined group of options. But those options in no way exhaust all the possibilities.

So, who limits your choices? You are only offered choices that everyone else finds acceptable. The only correct critical thinking conclusion is the options offered by someone else serve their best interests, and not necessarily yours.

If you don't like where you're heading, you must step out of the mainstream. You cannot limit your choices to the options someone else offers. You must *Think for Yourself.*

Prove to yourself that you are really free. Right now, think of something everyone does that is stupid. And right now choose to stop doing it.

We have to be realistic. We have to live in a society and admit we do not get to freely choose any options we want. But we can make many free will choices that aren't too anti-social. Right now, stop drinking soda pop. That's an undeniably good decision that puts you outside the mainstream. And it's one option you can offer to yourself rather than wait for someone else to make it available.

The internet is full of pretentious sounding "wisdom" relating choices to consequences. None of it actually helps you make choices. They just say things like "you are free to make choices but you cannot choose the consequences" or some variation on that.

Well, "duh" I guess. So you can choose to add one plus one, but you must accept the answer is two. A critical thinker does not need to read that on a T-shirt.

Critical thinkers make a decision because they want the consequences. In fact, the desired consequences are what drive their decision-making process. We are not passively accepting choices offered to us, we are actively seeking the best decisions. We do not let others define our choices.

Many choices you encounter on a path someone else controls are binary choices. Off or on. One or the other. This or that. Binary choices are the simplest to control and usually are an attempt to force you to continue living on someone else's terms. They are choosing the available paths. The consequences of your decision are already controlled between only two variables. And mostly they all lead back to the same path one way or another.

Binary choices present the illusion of a free will. *Don't Be Distracted.*

Define the Target. Binary. A numerical system having two as a base.

Our everyday number system is base 10. In base two, you have only 1 or 0. Almost everyone understands binary within the context of a transistor. It's either on or off. A simple binary device.

Life is not a transistor. Most good decisions in life are not binary. In addition to "on" and "off" we need a dimmer switch. Most bigger questions are not best answered with Yes or No. The universe of "Maybe" is far bigger.

Two lights can be ON at the same time. Two things can be true. Sometimes even three. In fact, many things can be true at the same time. Whenever you are pushed to choose between answers, first stop and consider if more than one can be true.

Then look for additional answers outside the two choices offered. Almost every goal has more than one correct answer. Why is the question presented as binary?

Usually someone pushing for a binary decision has a selfish reason. The universe of possible answers is usually much larger than two choices.

Simple example. You have a baby. Someone offers you Pampers or Luvs. They say Luvs are better but a little more expensive. Which do you want? A critical thinker immediately says "wait a minute". This does not have to be a binary choice. Among other options, there are cotton diapers and maybe even diaper services you may consider.

Before making a decision, you need to *Define the Target* further. What do I want from a diaper? Natural fibers? Disposable convenience. Lowest cost? The universe of choices is a lot bigger than a binary decision.

Proctor and Gamble owns both brands, Pampers and Luvs. They don't care which one you choose, but they'd love it if you accepted the binary choice offered.

That was an easy example. The problem with all binary decisions cannot be illustrated as simply as that one. But there is always some reason you are offered a binary decision instead of the whole universe of possibilities. A critical thinker wants the best answer, not just the better of two options chosen by someone else.

Diminishing Returns is a big part of *There Will Be Math*. Let's integrate it with binary decisions. Earlier we discussed feeding birds as an example of Diminishing Returns. Let's use that reference and transition it into a binary decision example.

Substitute the investment in any subsidy program to

help people rather than for feeding the birds. Immediately a critical thinker understands the problem to be solved with most social support programs. Just like the birds, too much aid and people forget how to feed themselves.

There is an optimal investment somewhere between always feeding the birds and never feeding them. There is no "on or off" solution. There is a "dimmer switch" answer. But many people involved in the debate represent it as a binary decision.

You get raging emotional debates going on. It's a complicated issue. Yet virtually every discussion deteriorates into a binary debate. It's either on or off. And neither "on" or "off" is the correct answer to a critical thinker.

Even the most hard-core conservative doesn't want to see people starving in the street. And the most liberal socialist understands some wealth must be created before it can be redistributed. Support for the less fortunate is a "dimmer switch" discussion among critical thinkers. If you ever expect to find the right answer, you have to look somewhere between "on or off". Real life is not a transistor.

This is supposed to be about critical thinking, not a political discussion. But politics affects everyone, and displays poor thinking on such a regular basis, it's just natural to choose it for examples.

The point is a good critical thinker will not allow themselves to be forced into a binary decision when neither choice is the right answer. Every time you are presented with a binary decision, first check for a third possible answer. Usually you will find the binary choice is being forced on you by someone with an agenda. The binary choice benefits them, not you. Always keep your "dimmer switch" ready.

There is a special category of binary decisions that are really no decision at all. This is the classic Hobson's choice scenario. Every critical thinker must be alert about spotting these before falling into the trap.

Note: The term "Hobson's choice" is credited to a stable owner who offered only one horse to each customer. The customer could take it or leave it. That story is probably better used as an example of supply and demand, but the name stuck and today a "Hobson's choice" is the same thing as "take it or leave it".

This "Hobson's" technique is most often used by pairing it with something impossible to ignore. You are presented with a problem which cannot be ignored and then expected to choose the proposed solution. Take it or leave it. This tactic is used everywhere. We would bore you to death and run into thousands of pages if we talked about all of them in detail.

But we need a few examples. So here are some terrible problems, all of which had bad answers proposed and adopted as the solution. To save space, we'll give you a problem and one bad answer that was adopted for each.

Zika virus, and billions spent for a vaccine. Global warming, and buying carbon offsets. Air travel safety, and creating the TSA. Gun violence, and police militarization. Terrorist threats, and spying on your emails. Budget deficits, and higher taxes. Personal debt crisis, and lower interest rates. Unemployment, and spending more on unemployment benefits. Drug addiction, and the War on Drugs. And on and on…

Critical thinkers can offer better answers for every one of those examples.

Here's a funny example. Or maybe this is a scary example. The USA has at least 15 different "intelligence" agencies. Each was offered as a solution to a very real problem, and so, of course, the agency had to be formed. It was the only answer.

Of course we need to know about foreign nuclear weapons. And so we need a new agency to do it. A critical thinker might say, "Wait a minute? Can't the CIA handle that?". But that wasn't offered as a choice.

In many cases, a dramatic problem can be recycled with a different answer proposed. In this way, many Hobson's choices can be forced by a single worthy problem. *Follow the Money*. The Hobson's "choice" being offered is always by someone who benefits from the solution being paired with it. Critical thinkers just decline to make the choice.

When confronted with a Hobson's choice, don't just think about the problem, always stop and ask yourself "Is the proposed answer right?" If not, then keep looking for the better answer. The opportunity cost of accepting wrong answers is huge. Every example listed above has a critical thinking answer that is more effective for less cost. In many cases, accepting the bad answers is actually killing people.

Let's pick the latest world-ending disease and use it for

example. As we write this, the best data we can find shows Zika virus has been blamed for about 5,000 cases of birth defects world-wide. Most of the various countries reporting also have some deaths attributed. Maybe 1,000 deaths total. That's if you believe all the malnourished mothers have only mosquitos to blame... and the unhealthy 75-year-old in Puerto Rico really died from his mosquito bite. Bad statistics, all, but the problem is real so let's just accept the BS, for now, to help make the following critical thinking point.

There will be roughly 200 million cases of malaria next year. And there have been that many for many years prior. Hundreds of thousands will die from malaria next year. Malaria has been killing a lot of people for a long time. In fact, mosquito-borne diseases have killed tens of millions since tracking began. And the birth defects caused by mosquito-borne disease have never really been counted.

So which mosquito problem should be in the headlines?

The point is not to say Zika isn't a bad thing. The point is to use critical thinking and see the flaw in accepting a forced decision. This is presented as an emergency and we have to do something!

Wait a minute. The opportunity cost of such a choice is too high. In this case, malaria will kill millions more while the world fixates on a much smaller problem. *Learn from History*. This same tactic has been used for Bird flu, swine flu, legionnaire's disease, Ebola, HIV, the war on communism, the war on drugs, Saddam Hussein... the list goes on and on.

There really are some tragic problems out there. It would be great to allocate resources based on critical thinking rather than the latest PR bullshit. Try to get inside the head of someone showing you pictures of deformed babies. Why are they doing that?

Follow the Money. If you pick almost any press release from the WHO (World Health Organization) you will find scary statements that eventually lead to them needing more money. In their own press releases, you can read about new diseases being discovered at an alarming rate.

Critical thinking question. Are these diseases new? Were these an emergency before, or after WHO named them? Why are new diseases being discovered at an alarming rate? Has the world suddenly become so unhealthy?

Follow the Money. Drug companies get paid to research. And government funds most of it. Funding is limited, and agencies have to compete for it. As we write this, the USA government alone is considering $2 billion in emergency funding for Zika research. (Critical thinkers will appreciate some irony here; part of that budget is coming from unclaimed money previously approved for Ebola research.)

Side note: The Gates Foundation has donated over $2 billion to malaria research. Wow. A capitalist who understands capitalism. Go Bill! Consider running for president...

Don't Be Distracted. Businesses and bureaucracies want money. They will use whatever disease gets your attention. And the Hobson's choice offered is between funding them or accepting more deformed babies. Don't accept binary choices. There are always other more effective answers possible.

Our goal is always to be like the child in the Emperor's New Clothes. See everything through your own eyes, *Think for Yourself* and don't see only what someone else tells you is there.

24.
Interlude: Bad Decision #2

LET'S STAY WITH the medical industry for another example of bad decision-making.

We will use knee surgery here. Specifically, surgery to repair cartilage damage or meniscus tears. There are roughly 1 million procedures performed each year at an average cost of around $10,000. We don't need to be very precise here. Conservatively it's a $10 billion market.

There is zero data proving any benefits. In fact...

Wait a minute! This is starting to sound familiar? *Learn from History*. That's right! It's the same scenario as bad decision number one.

But you see? Critical thinking patterns repeat over and over. You become a "quick-thinker" because you recognize them. You skip to the end.

If you do this enough, inevitably you will annoy some people with your "aggressiveness". When that happens, you will have to explain you're not being aggressive, you've just been here before and skipped ahead a little.

Always be nice when dealing with people who are not "quick-thinkers". You have to wait for them to catch up.

25.
Putting It All Together

LET'S DO SOME real life critical thinking examples. We'll pick some topics here that touch a lot of people. Even if these do not involve you directly, you are certainly touching someone who is impacted by these examples.

This is an advanced concepts book, so these are going to challenge the *Open Mind* more than simple questions. The more interesting questions do not have easy answers. But critical thinking will keep the debate within the boundaries of what would make a good decision.

The application of the other ten critical thinking principles requires a deeper commitment here too. Emotion competes with critical thinking for your brain space. Emotions challenge your intellectual honesty. But in the end, your emotions will be happier if your critical thinking makes the decisions.

The most interesting questions have no empirical answer. All we can do is use critical thinking, hope for some synergy in discussions with other critical thinkers, and then determine the best answer available.

These examples include more of my point of view than I'd like. I really just want to illustrate critical thinking. So remember it's always OK to disagree, as long as your process is intellectually honest. In fact, I love to hear intellectually honest disagreements. It's how a critical thinker learns something new. But remember emotions don't count. Emotions carry zero weight in a critical thinking process. Answers don't change based on how you feel about them.

Try not to get bogged down in the specific topics. Many other topics can be substituted for the examples chosen here. The point of the exercise is to become a better critical thinker. Learn the techniques and make them a habit. You can disagree with my point of view on everything, just use critical thinking to do it. Like I said, these were chosen to challenge. It's easy to think about things you like. It's much harder to use critical thinking on topics you "feel" strongly about.

OK, let's start with one that should test almost everyone's intellectual honesty.

The vast majority of people in the world accept the theory of evolution. But, there is a resolute minority who do not. The debate is largely a binary choice. You believe or you don't. And unfortunately, the debate rarely uses critical thinking.

Life is not a binary choice. To be an intellectually honest critical thinker, you must have a "dimmer switch" view of this debate. Let's start with the graphic that follows:

That scene is not supported by critical thinking. It's just a theory without data supporting it. To the extent it represents evolution as a general concept, it might be OK to use. Like the graphics on bathroom doors are OK to indicate the boys or girls room. But I don't want evolution shown this way in any school science books. There is no data that has met any generally accepted standard of proof. It's not real enough to be taught as a science.

Many of you might be laughing at me now. That's why we put the practical examples at the end... Anyway, remember, *Open Mind* and stay intellectually honest. That's why I chose this example. *Open Mind* is the most important principle. Critical thinking is of little value if you'll only accept the answers you like.

Ready? Here's one critical thinker's analysis of evolution theory.

There is plenty of good data available to show living organisms evolve. The evidence is real and the tests repeatable. Evolution of living organisms through natural selection has met the standard of proof required to be considered a fact.

To suggest evolution does not exist is intellectually

dishonest. So if you want to argue for "intelligent design", "creationism" or similar ideas, you must include the fact that living organisms still evolve after their initial creation.

Respect Nature. The only rational argument is about the starting point for evolution, and not whether or not it exists. You cannot deny evolution exists in nature.

However, there are limits to the proofs. Moths evolve quickly for their survival. Mice evolve quickly in the lab too. Bacteria evolve so quickly antibiotics cannot keep up.

But evolution within a species is all that's been proven. One species has never been evolved into another species in a laboratory. Bacteria have never grown into frogs. Reptiles have never become mice. And mice have never become monkeys. There is no repeatable test data to prove the evolution of any complex species from a simpler one.

So, can a critical thinker really get too impassioned trying to defend the idea "we all came out of the swamp"? What would be the objective basis for that argument? Evolutionists are required to be intellectually honest too.

The biggest, and some would argue most important, parts of evolutionary theory have no data at all to prove them. We are a long way from any proof a single cell organism evolved into all the life on earth today. Nothing has ever proven my ancestors include some amphibian from a billion years ago. It's all just a theory.

To demand people believe evolution works like that is intellectually dishonest. It has not met the standards of proof one would demand for even a poorly supported food or drug safety claim.

Additionally, no matter how far back you push the theory of evolution, at some point you have to address the beginning. The main point of the question posed by "Intelligent Design" theorists is equally valid whether you place them a billion years ago or just 11,000 years ago. What started that first living organism? Are we back to spontaneous generation again?

Evolution of us all starting from a single cell somewhere is an interesting theory. And no more. Everything else is just people talking and their emotional reactions.

And our final point on this issue. As we discussed earlier, advanced critical thinkers understand many questions cannot be answered. The fact a question has not been answered does not make any proposed answer today more correct. This is another Hobson's choice. We don't know what caused the first living organism, but if the choice is between no answer and a bad answer, critical thinking must conclude there is no reason to make the choice at all.

We can carry this point one step further and address a more practical question. This one does need an answer. What do we teach young students in school? The side carrying the most votes has been winning that kind of argument for a long time.

But wouldn't it be better to teach science with intellectual honesty attached? Wouldn't it be better to admit science tries too hard to explain things it cannot prove, to admit science has made many mistakes in the past, and teach people it's a good idea to have an *Open Mind* in case some new information comes along?

For a critical thinker, the only answer to the evolution debate is there is not very much to debate. We don't have many facts and we really don't know the answers. An advanced critical thinker accepts the limitations of available knowledge and spends their time on other problems. Basing too many decisions on an unproven theory is not the way to make a life great.

OK, let's look at a completely different type of example. Everyone is involved with money somehow. Let's analyze something to do with money.

What do you think about the minimum wage debates? From your observations, do you see a lot of critical thinking attached? Let's do some right now.

Define the Target. Minimum wage – The lowest wage permitted by law, or by agreement between employer and employees as with a union.

The question is a hot political topic in the USA as we write this. But some good critical thinking on a question can last forever, so let's try to keep this analysis timeless. Whenever a topic comes up, you won't spend much time thinking on it if you've previously worked out the right answer.

Where does a critical thinker start on minimum wage? *First Things First.* Much of the debate seems to be about whether or not we should have a minimum wage. That is not intellectually honest. We have one. No one is asking anyone if you think we should have one. That debate was over the first time a minimum wage law was enacted. An intellectually honest critical thinker will not confuse two different questions. The only question open for debate is what the wage should be.

Two things can be true. You can passionately say you don't think we should have any minimum wage at all and still work on setting the minimum wage. You have to admit the society has already made the decision. You believe differently but lost. Get over it. Now your job is to set the wage appropriately.

That really appears to be the hardest part of the minimum wage debate - getting everyone to address the right question. Remember, we call that *Define the Target*.

Define the Target. Exactly what is our goal in this debate? Setting the minimum wage.

Anything not addressing that goal is a distraction. *Don't Be Distracted*. When someone says we shouldn't have one, just say "that's not the question" and don't waste any more bandwidth on whatever their arguments. If you want to be nicer, say "we can have that debate later over cocktails, but it's not why we're here right now."

Two things can be true. You can be against minimum wage as a concept, and still set an intellectually honest minimum wage. *Learn from History*. That level of critical thinking is beyond most politicians. But, history has shown that just a few good thinkers can move an entire government. We don't need all politicians to be smart, just a few good leaders would be enough.

OK, for purposes of our critical thinking example here, we already have a minimum wage and the only relevant question is, what should it be? I'd approach it this way. Remember "WIC" from our first day getting in critical thinking shape? The first question is always "Why?".

So... Why? What is the purpose of a minimum wage? Why did we make it a law? The wage we set needs to meet the intended purpose of the law.

Pretty much universally accepted, the rationale behind a minimum wage law is this: anyone who works in good faith for someone else deserves to receive a living wage in return. And, since we cannot rely on businesses to act in good faith, we will make a law that requires employers to pay what the government determines. (Sorry all you good-faith businesses. A few bad apples spoiled it for everyone... now it's law.)

There is no point in having the law if it does not fulfill its purpose. If government officials do not set a minimum wage in accordance with the law's purpose, then they have failed to fulfill their obligations to the law. A minimum wage must be set that is an intellectually honest "living wage".

Answer part one. Minimum wage must be indexed to inflation. *There Will Be Math*. If you're already at a minimum wage, and then your costs go up, by definition your current wage must now be below the minimum. Not keeping minimum wage up with inflation is intellectually dishonest. And, once done, then this part of the minimum wage question would be answered once and go away forever. What could politicians do with all that time saved in the future?

In further support of that conclusion, Social Security is indexed to inflation. *Simplify*. It's easy to tie minimum wage to the same index. Social security payments went up 2% this year? So does minimum wage. Simple. No more time wasted discussing it ever again.

Answer part two. Get rid of the bullshit. All the discussions over higher minimum wage costing the economy jobs etc. are just emotional rhetoric. There is no data showing a higher minimum wage causes an economy to lose jobs. In fact, data suggests the contrary. I would not call it conclusive proof, but the data points to wage hikes being followed by increased consumption which in turn causes economic growth.

Follow the Money. Without digressing too far into how money really works, we have to make one "money nerd" fact clear here. Money spent grows an economy more than money saved. One effective way to grow an economy is to route more money to the people who spend it. Rich people do not spend all their money. People living on minimum wage spend every penny they make. (Read our book "Don't be Stupid about Money" for more in-depth on this topic.)

So far we've decided minimum wage needs to rise with inflation, and minimum wage spenders are probably good for the economy. Those seem pretty easy to me. Numbers are always the easiest to think about critically. The next part is harder.

Answer part three. What is the fundamentally correct living wage? There are a lot of ideals involved here. We have to start out knowing this cannot be an entirely data-driven analysis. Data can help quite a bit, but the answer also depends on how much economic inequality a society wants to accept.

We can start by defining some boundaries. Data has proven that total income equality does not work. Data has also proven that too much inequality fails just as badly. We won't take the space here to offer all the ways data proves those boundaries, we'll just *Learn from History*. Income inequality in France led to Louis the XVI losing his head. And the failure of communism in pretty much every country that tried it demonstrated people need some financial incentive in order to work hard and create wealth. So with failures defining the bookends, the right answer must be somewhere in between.

Although we cannot carry the critical thinking through to an empirical answer, we can take some guidance from past capitalists. *Learn from History*. Andrew Carnegie was an amazing capitalist. You can read his "Gospel of Wealth" on our website. We would never have needed minimum wage laws if certain people could live forever.

We can also look to modern day capitalists for guidance. John Mackey of Whole Foods and Conscious Capitalism is one good example. John Bogle and Vanguard is another. Both of these men created enormous benefits for other people while they themselves also became very rich. John and Jack are very different people, yet accomplished very similar goals. And they raised the bar at all their competitors as well. The economic benefit people like this bring to a society is impossible to calculate.

Both of their companies are around $12 per hour minimum right now, along with excellent employee benefits. Total compensation value received by their lowest paid employees is probably around $14 per hour.

Simplify. I'm not going to out-think two iconic capitalists. I'm going with $14 per hour, or the equivalent with benefits included, as my recommendation for minimum wage. It clearly allows the people at the top to get very wealthy while also providing a decent life for everyone going to work in their companies. And this wage would be indexed to the cost of living, raising it exactly the same percentage as Social Security benefits paid each year.

And we're done. We never have to debate minimum wage again. Critical thinking makes this a pretty easy discussion. And it makes life very efficient.

Now, if you still want to revisit the question of whether or not there should be a minimum wage law at all, that point is also worthy of discussion. It's intellectually honest for me to say minimum wage should be $14 per hour, but I don't think we should have laws about it at all. All of the people mentioned above we looked to for guidance, dead and alive, they all pretty much agree government regulation makes things worse.

Government regulations create "crony capitalism". It's bad for the people, and we don't have the space to continue that analysis here. We'll just point out that China executes politicians engaging in similar behavior. I'd settle for just not re-electing them...

Anyway, we set our minimum wage and no blood was shed thanks to Critical Thinking.

Time for one more? We've already picked on the medical industry for a couple of our bad decision examples. But medical care is a big part of many people's lives, so let's do one more. We will do this one in greater depth than the surgery examples.

Way too many people are taking prescription drugs today. Let's do a little critical thinking about it.

Follow the Money. Healthcare accounts for about 18% of the total economic activity in the USA. In most other advanced economies, it's around 11%. The total amount of money paid is one of those numbers too big to comprehend. A reasonable estimate is about $9 trillion. Drug revenue alone is over $1 trillion. *Common Sense* alarm bell immediately starts ringing. When that much money is involved, all critical thinkers know *Follow the Money* must be used in an analysis.

We will use one prescription drug category here as the example to exercise our critical thinking. Statins. Crestor, Lipitor, Zocor, Pravachol and various others - they're all statin drugs with minor differences primarily useful for marketing departments.

Perhaps nowhere else in the health care arena has it been more important for critical thinkers to use *Follow the Money* and *There Will Be Math*.

Statins are another sad example of a good idea gone bad. We will avoid a detailed discussion on the pharmacology here. There's too much data to put in one little book. *Simplify*. The data is not clear enough to prove any answers. The world is full of opposing points of view, usually stated with great passion.

People get emotionally involved in something they put in their body every day. But people really get emotionally involved in the profits these drugs generate. The debate rarely stays within the boundaries of good critical thinking.

First, let's *Trust Common Sense*. When so many smart people fail to agree, then the answer cannot be easy. We must be intellectually honest and conclude we cannot get a data-driven empirical answer. Therefore, we use *Open Mind* and take in all the information available.

First a brief summary. A correlation between high cholesterol and heart disease was first suggested in the early 1900's and later on became pretty well supported by good studies in the 1950's. A correlation means two things occur together; it does not mean one causes the other.

Critical thinking mistake number one: an industry was born around reducing your cholesterol. Unfortunately, this was based only on a correlation. There was no proof of cause and effect. But a mega-blockbuster industry was born around reducing your cholesterol.

In 1960 no one took statin drugs because they did not exist. Today "guidelines" in the USA say roughly 60% of all people should be taking them. Time for a critical thinker's *Common Sense* alarm bell to go off. Zero to 60? Really?

Some inventions deserve a high and rapid rate of adoption. That happens when the benefits are clear and people stampede toward the product. Think CD's replacing vinyl records. Sometimes the stampede is a mistake. Think CD's replacing Vinyl records...

Anyway, the stampede to statins was driven by fear and advertising. It correlates with drug companies starting to advertise direct to the public. Drug companies are very effective advertisers. Unfortunately, the products they advertise are potent and potentially dangerous drugs.

As we write this, only the USA and New Zealand allow direct to public advertising of statins. *Follow the Money*. Direct to consumer advertising by drug companies is a more than $3 billion industry.

To counter all that advertising, another brief summary of available data will help.

Your body needs cholesterol. You would die without it. Your body makes cholesterol as needed. We do not rely on eating it. If you need less you make less, and if you need more you make more. Primarily your liver handles this function.

If you take a statin, you are interfering with your body's normal action. Your body makes what you need. The drug stops it. *Respect Nature* is immediately causing me serious concerns here.

Statins are powerful drugs and many people taking them suffer undesirable side effects, including premature death. *There Will Be Math*. The return on investment has to be clear enough to make risks like that worthwhile.

Unfortunately, there is only that original correlation. Data proving any benefits from using a drug to reduce cholesterol in the blood simply does not exist. For the vast majority of people taking statins, there is just no data showing it has any benefits.

Does any of this sound familiar? If not, please go back

and re-read bad decision examples number one and two, right now. *Learn from History*. We've been here before. Critical thinkers are ready for this.

Let's use *Common Sense* again. Do you really think 60% of all Americans need a drug therapy to interfere with their body's normal actions? Maybe we should *Respect Nature* a little more. Only at the peak of hubris could someone suggest nature gets it wrong 60% of the time. Every good critical thinker knows this, if we fight nature 60% of the time, then losing is inevitable.

So how did we get from no one taking statins in 1960, to recommendation 60% of people take statins today? That should be obvious to a critical thinker by now. *Follow the Money*. The profits are a number too big to relate to. And then just continue on with the analysis same as in our medical industry bad decision examples one and two. It's just a repeat of the same process.

But let's also look from another critical thinking direction. *Learn from History*. Is it reliable when big Pharma and/or big Government agencies make these kinds of recommendation? Have these institutions been so accurate and honest in the past that now we trust them? It scares me that question needs to be asked. I really don't want to learn people have gotten that stupid.

I have to use this again: *Simplify*. We like George Carlin's guidance here. "I don't believe anything the government tells me. Nothing. Zero." Right after government, we'd add big business. George also has some great quotes on that, but we're not doing his biography here.

Learn from History. These are the same people who told you not to eat eggs or shrimp because of their cholesterol content; to reduce butter consumption and use margarine instead; don't fry in beef fat. And after years of ignoring real evidence, years of rationalizing and wasting our time, they've finally started to admit they were wrong.

For the record; There is not now, and never was, any evidence proving that eating foods containing cholesterol is bad for you. In fact, much of the advice to avoid those foods really was bad for you. For example, as good studies and reliable data come in: margarine turns out to be very bad for you (trans fats) and most vegetable oils burn at low temperatures becoming carcinogenic where beef tallow would not. Egg eaters turned out to be healthier than those who never ate eggs. And this list could go on for a long time...

The point is, given their track record, why would people believe government or big pharma recommendations when they say take statins if your cholesterol is over 200?

I have enough data to predict the income of the drug companies when their statin sales go up. There is plenty of data available for that. But there is no data available to calculate any health benefit to all the people paying for those drugs.

As it stands today, there is still zero evidence that high cholesterol in an otherwise healthy person has any effect on cardiovascular health. In fact, even that original correlation with heart disease has been narrowed to something more specific. High cholesterol only correlates with heart disease if you smoke, are obese, sedentary, diabetic or otherwise unhealthy. So even the correlation that started the whole industry turns out to be more narrow than originally thought.

In fact, if you parse the data to remove those with cholesterol over 325, you end up with nothing at all. No correlations, nothing at all useful to a critical thinking discussion.

Eliminating the extremes is a common practice depending on what you want to learn from your statistics. Extremes can distort the more useful data. For example, you don't include the two mansions costing millions if you want to consider the average housing price among hundreds of other houses in an area you plan to move into.

There Will Be Math. In the world of medical statistics, it's quite common to include the extremes, include those who are the very sickest and then extrapolate that data into the averages for a general population. It's bad statistics. It's BS.

You could make a fair case for saying cholesterol over 350 indicates statins might help. But the problem is those honest numbers don't offer a big enough market. So the bullshit begins and then you get the number down to 200. Now that's a number where some serious revenue can be generated! 60% of the population is a nice-sized target market for a big company. 1% is too small. They have to aim higher.

Whenever you are part of a target market, immediately picture the bullseye on your back.

Don't Be Distracted. Numbers only mean something if

used to explain something else. And there are no studies or reliable statistics saying a number of 200 for your cholesterol means anything. Not even 300 means anything.

There is one area of cardiovascular study with very good data. Exercise is a proven therapy that can help your heart. There are good studies in this area from which you can draw real conclusions. Even people promoting statin use accept this data. Actually, they're forced to include it in their sales pitch. "When diet and exercise aren't enough", etc.

Active people have lower rates of cardiovascular disease. There is no "high" cholesterol number that means anything in this group. In fact, there is evidence lower than average cholesterol is bad for athletic performance. And there is some evidence that cholesterol below 180 correlates with premature death.

Bottom line, if you are a healthy and active person, you have no reason to even know your cholesterol number. There's nothing useful it can tell you. *Think for Yourself.* Thinking about cholesterol is a waste of your bandwidth. Your body takes care of it the same as digesting breakfast. Use the time you save to think about something else to make your life better.

If you're obese or diabetic, then maybe you should include "high" cholesterol in your health concerns too. But in that case, getting some exercise offers a far more tested and proven way to gain reliable benefits. *Think for Yourself.* Just go for a nice walk every day. It's proven to do more for you than statin drugs. Plus, you can use the time to think about other things to make your life better. You can critical think and walk at the same time. Artificially low cholesterol is actually bad for brain function.

Unfortunately, if you do not *Think for Yourself*, other people will think for you. *Follow the Money*. It's never best for you when someone else making money is also making decisions for you.

We started this discussion by saying statins are an example of a good idea gone bad. Even though they've been abused and people are being killed in the pursuit of bigger profits, we must still use *Open Mind* on the subject.

There Will Be Math. There is good evidence statins may prolong life and reduce incidence of heart attacks in high-risk patients. High-risk patients who legitimately fear an imminent heart attack should consider taking a statin drug. Even here, the number itself doesn't mean too much. There are other indicators of imminent heart attack that are more useful in prescribing statins.

Statins should be a drug category that saves lives. In the right patients, they work. That's maybe 1% of the population at most. But *Follow the Money*. Greed is a powerful force. Bad statistics and fear are easy to sell to stupid people. Making 60 times more money looks possible to drug companies.

There is another *Follow the Money* issue with statins worth mentioning. In the very litigious US health care system, the best way to avoid losing a lawsuit is to follow the accepted "standard of care". Unfortunately, statins are passing the tipping point. Any doctor using their own common sense or "dimmer switch" may find themselves at odds with the prevailing standard of care. Financially, it's just safer to recommend statins if your patient's cholesterol is over 200. It's sad. I feel bad for doctors who want to use *Think for Yourself*. The only way to solve that dilemma is if enough patients engage in some critical thinking.

Health care, in general, is in desperate need of critical thinking. We chose statins for an example because they are familiar to most people and offer such a wide range of possibilities to demonstrate critical thinking. But there are many smaller selling drugs on the market with stunningly bad statistics supporting their claims. These drugs harm many people while offering no real benefits, just profits to their companies.

Think for Yourself. Critical thinking is needed more than ever when your health is involved. No one else is really motivated to keep you healthy. They're motivated to sell you products and services. You are the only one who will think critically about your health care.

Well, that concludes our three real world examples. We covered evolution, minimum wage, and statin drugs. If we all did our job together, you should not have to think about them again unless some game-changing new data materializes.

Here's one more; The life expectancy of a healthy 65 year-old living in Hawaii is about 25% longer than in Mississippi. Why is that?

Simplify. I don't want to analyze it. I just want to move to Hawaii.

Answering questions with critical thinking makes life very efficient.

26.
Bonus Principle: Time is Even More Priceless

THE THING ABOUT time is this: the less time you have, the more you appreciate it.

If we could get everyone to integrate that into daily thinking, a lot less stupidity would happen in this world. Does anyone really want to trade a single precious moment of their life on stupidity? Probably not, but first they have to be aware of it.

And based on a quick look around, it's clear a whole lot of people are not aware of the time they're wasting. Way too many people are trading away precious time on being stupid. But critical thinkers are not in that herd. *Time is Priceless* to us.

Certain decisions don't matter much. Eating the potato salad at a picnic is usually a bad decision. But most likely the time wasted will be a few trips to the bathroom and maybe a poor night's sleep. Time-saving note: *Simplify.* Mayonnaise is always a bad decision unless you know its entire history.

Knowing the potential time cost of a decision should automatically kick in your critical thinking. It's a habit. Know the time cost and add critical thinking accordingly. You cannot get wasted time back again.

And time is what you need the most of to make your life great.

There are decisions with more potential time lost than mayo. If you make a bad housing decision, you will suffer with it a long time. Maybe 30 years or more if it involves a mortgage. We've discussed critical thinking and the financial benefits elsewhere. Here, let's just take note of the time cost.

Getting married? Let's deflate the romance for a moment and notice this decision is going to involve a lot of time. Use critical thinking. Is there real synergy in the relationship? A lifetime of synergy, as opposed to antipathy, adds an incalculable amount of time back into a life.

Want some children? That's a lot of time. Buying anything with debt? Hope you enjoy the time spent with payments. Examples can go on and on, but the point is a critical thinker understands *Time is Priceless* and includes it in decision making.

Kicking the concept up to a more advanced level, critical thinkers don't waste their time with intellectual dishonesty. We mentioned this earlier. *Define the Target*. Intellectual dishonesty – Failure to apply rational standards of which one is aware. This is a real time waster.

People routinely distort facts or even just lie in an effort to make their point. And of course, they are outraged when the other side does the same thing. These people waste everyone's time. A critical thinker insists on intellectual honesty. We cannot allow stupidity to waste our time. I want the right answer ASAP. *Time is*

Priceless.

Easy example: I don't care what your political views, the debate over Obama's birth certificate was intellectually dishonest. Critical thinkers spent zero time on it. Critical thinkers who want a different president choose more honest issues to pursue. If all those stupid people chasing birth certificates had spent their precious time wisely, maybe the next election would have reflected more of their views.

More to the point, with some critical thinking maybe we'd elect a government that accomplishes something regardless of who is president or what political party is in charge. Bad government wastes way too much of our priceless time. Everyone should be angry about it. But we elect them, so we have to take responsibility too.

Time is a finite resource. Critical thinking is a way we can get more from the time we have. We can even make decisions that get us a little more time. Prioritizing personal health is a good start. Just eating right and sleeping well is a good start.

There is incredible technology available for health. Instead of billion dollar drugs we don't need, maybe some critical thinking could channel all that money and talent toward something more useful. Who knows, maybe Google and their longevity project will get it done. Or maybe the Gates foundation. But imagine if all the energy put into bad BS from big Pharma was also pointed in the right direction.

We don't have enough time in our life to waste any on stupidity. Making good decisions is the only way we can get more time in our lives.

How much time can you gain by being a critical thinker? How much time can you add back into your life? It only depends on how long you keep it going. Critical thinking results compound. Answers build on each other. Each step is easier because the last step helped it along.

The less time we spend on any decision, the more time we have for something else. Some good decisions make your life longer. Some make your life better. Critical thinking gives you infinitely more time to pursue both.

Critical thinking itself is another good example of a counter-intuitive truth. The more advanced your application of the principles, the simpler your life becomes.

27.
Closing Remarks

CRITICAL THINKING IS not difficult. You can start using our principles to analyze the stupidity around you right away. Combining them will give you even more power. And practice will make you very fast at using them.

Critical thinking sometimes takes a long time. Sometimes you might get tired and say to yourself "I don't want to think that much". That's OK. Just leave it and come back later. It's not the time to make that decision. Come back to it when you feel like thinking some more. Whatever you do, don't rush into a bad decision.

We'll repeat a summary of our principles here:

Your *Open Mind* can quickly accept the best answers. That means you can use the rest of the time for something better. Or you can spend a lot of brainpower trying to rationalize wrong beliefs. Don't let emotions keep you from an *Open Mind*.

First Things First. Don't waste time on decisions with no impact. Quit smoking now and live longer. Move on to good diet and exercise. If you're already there, move on to getting happier. Keep prioritizing decisions that compound into the future.

Respect Nature. Know your place in the universe. Do

not spit into the wind.

Don't Be Distracted. You can make decisions based only on the data that matters. You can look at all the pretty pictures too, just don't let them influence a decision.

Define Your Target and get to the point. Don't waste time when everyone isn't addressing the same goal.

Common Sense must be given a chance to work. Going too fast will ignore it. And going too fast will miss anything counterintuitive.

You can waste hours tracking your spending every month. Or *There Will Be Math.* You can do it right once and maximize your return on investment (shameless plug - read "Don't Be Stupid about Money"). Then use those hours you save each month to do something else.

You can *Follow the Money* and quickly decide if information is valid.

You can *Simplify*, saving yourself time and making decisions easier. Simplifying makes life very efficient.

Learn from History and make decisions quickly because you recognize the question. One good analysis can last a lifetime.

Most of all, you can step away from the herd and *Think for Yourself.* Do not waste your life doing what everyone else does. What would be the point?

And when you start combining all those principles to attack a problem, the thinking power rises exponentially.

Critical thinking sounds harder than it is. Even when advancing the concepts, always remember to *Simplify*.

Make Confucius proud. There is absolutely nothing out there that cannot be reduced to simple terms. Even critical thinking.

Choose your way to a great life.

Think long and prosper.

28.
Don't Be Stupid Club

AT DONTBESTUPID.CLUB WE help make the world a little less stupid.

We think critically. We start with an *Open Mind*. Then we apply our principles and think about the question. A little critical thinking is all that's required to quickly reach most answers. Sometimes a little more work is required. But we always get to the answer.

We really don't care what people think. But we do care about how they think. Any well-reasoned opinion deserves respect. And opinions without basis are just stupid. Differing answers are fine as long as critical thinking is used. If you hate our answer and have a well-reasoned opposition, GREAT! Maybe we will learn something from you.

We're all in this adventure together. We're stupid too. We are all conditioned from birth to think the wrong way. Everyone with something to gain would prefer you just stampede in the direction of what they say. But hopefully we are a little less stupid for trying to fix that.

Critical thinking is a skill that can be learned. It's not even a difficult skill. It's harder to be a good welder or good coder or good baseball player. It's impossible for most of us to dunk a basketball. But we all can be good thinkers.

Critical thinking is a way of looking at the world. It's a framework for thinking about anything. You're going to spend time thinking anyway, why not make the most of it? We think life is easier this way. You never feel lost if you know how to think.

Most disagreements we observe just come from people violating our principles. Arguing points without defining their targets... adding complexity to hide their own inadequacies... trying to bullshit their way to a profit... going against nature... doing the wrong things first... all just stupid.

The world can be a much better place if we are all a little less stupid.

And know this. If you think critically, then you are never stupid. The stupidity is all around you, but it can never get YOU! Critical thinking is stronger than stupidity. Answers always equal power.

Our goal is to make a little difference in your life and entertain. Let us know how we did. We'd love to hear from you.

We don't play any of the review games (less than 50% of reviews happen organically these days) so you will see fewer reviews for our books. If you choose to leave one, it will be more meaningful and we sincerely appreciate it. If you hate anything I'd rather your write me personally so we can discuss it.

Visit http://DontBeStupid.club if you'd like more.

Our Amazon Store is located at: http://astore.amazon.com/dontbclub-20. It's where you'll find some of the products we like. Nothing in our store is stupid. You don't pay anything extra, but we get a little commission if you buy here. And we appreciate it. It helps keep making the world a little less stupid.

Thank you for investing your time with us.

53234324R00089

Made in the USA
San Bernardino, CA
10 September 2017